The Restless School

Roy Blatchford

 A John Catt Publication

First Published 2014
This edition published 2015
by John Catt Educational Ltd,
12 Deben Mill Business Centre, Old Maltings Approach,
Melton, Woodbridge IP12 1BL

Tel: +44 (0) 1394 389850 Fax: +44 (0) 1394 386893
Email: enquiries@johncatt.com
Website: www.johncatt.com

Opinions expressed in this publication are those of the contributors
and are not necessarily those of the publishers or the editors.
We cannot accept responsibility for any errors or omissions.

ISBN: 978 1 909717 07 7

Set and designed by John Catt Educational Limited

Printed and bound in Great Britain
by Ashford Colour Press.

What four leaders say about *The Restless School*

How often do you come across a book about education that puts in a nutshell all the things you've so often thought but never managed entirely to articulate? Roy Blatchford has written just such a book. But *The Restless School* is in no way cosy or predictable. On the contrary, it is deeply challenging to anyone - classroom teacher, school leader, policy-maker - who is prepared to read it thoughtfully and honestly. Drawing on his lifetime of experience he defines more neatly than I've encountered anywhere else the 'common purpose' and 'unchanging values' of schools, and thus of those who work in them.

Bernard Trafford MA MEd PhD FRSA
Headmaster, Royal Grammar School, Newcastle

I felt totally challenged, inspired and motivated by the author's passion for children being at the very heart of schools. This book is a must read for those who feel drawn to the possibility of joining the teaching profession as well as for those of us who are seasoned professionals or policy-makers. It provides a wonderful opportunity for reflection. Roy Blatchford reminds us of the moral purpose that we need to keep sight of in this ever changing educational landscape and that all schools should strive to be 'restless'!

Ava Sturridge-Packer CBE
Executive Headteacher: St Mary's Church of England Primary and Nursery Academy, St Michael's of England Primary Academy, Birmingham

Expect to be stopped in your tracks when you read this. Thought-provoking, wise and challenging - I loved it!

Alison Peacock DBE
Headteacher, The Wroxham School

Roy Blatchford draws on 40 years of wide-ranging experience within the UK and international education systems in order to capture the essence of successful schools. The image of schools which are 'restless to improve' - never complacent, however successful, founded on a 'crucible of values' - provides a deeply positive and optimistic vision of a thriving and confident education service.

Brian Lightman
General Secretary, Association of School and College Leaders (ASCL)

For Anne and Luke

All men dream: but not equally.
Those who dream by night in the dusty
recesses of their minds wake in the day
to find that it was vanity: but the dreamers
of the day are dangerous men, for they may
act their dreams with open eyes, to make it
possible.

T.E. Lawrence, *The Seven Pillars of Wisdom*

Contents

Chapter 1

Assertions

Youth is a circumstance you can't do anything about. The trick is to grow up without getting old.

Frank Lloyd Wright

We who teach are no different from those in other walks of life: to be motivated, challenged, and occasionally inspired keeps the spirits high.

I am an impatient optimist, often in thrall to dangerous ideas. I have been writing this book all my working life and intend to keep on writing it. In many ways, the narrative reflects my own 'school journey' though 40 years of teaching, leading and inspecting schools, and being an observer of the politics and practice of education. I wanted this book to draw together the essence of what I have written and spoken about schooling in many contexts.

The German writer and politician Goethe memorably observed: 'Everything has been thought of before - the challenge is to think of it again.' Through the chapters I seek to offer some fresh (if not new) perspectives for those who teach in and lead our schools and school systems, alongside identifying pointers for continuing and renewed success. I make a few assertions and indulge in futures thinking too. The book concludes with an historical perspective: writings selected from my published archive which attest to my thinking and practice over time.

This is a book rooted in a UK perspective, so the use of 'we' and 'our' in the text frequently refers to systems of education operating in this kingdom, particularly England. Equally, I have called on my extensive professional experiences in different parts of the world, so trust that the text will have something to offer to a broader diaspora of teachers and school leaders.

I once heard the celebrated film-maker Woody Allen say that 80% of success is showing up, so thank you for opening the book thus far. Let me begin by making a few assertions to hook you in:

- In common with other government-funded public services, state schools in the UK are in better health now than they were in 1973 when I started teaching in Brixton, London.

- So too are UK independent schools, motivated by changing social norms and the ever-increasing expectations of fee-paying parents.

- And so too are international schools across the globe, driven by international benchmarking and inspection frameworks which relentlessly raise the bar.

- After decades of focused international research and practice, we know today what successful schools look, smell and feel like.

- We know what works in school improvement, and we know what failure looks like.

- School systems across the world are ever in search of 'the gold standard'; thus all governments urge their respective education systems to 'be above average' (an ever-rising 'average'), and to compete with the best.

- If one significant international measure of educational success and of the schooling system is entry to higher education, more young people enter university than ever before, and that rising tide is inexorable.

The text is written with the quiet certainty that whatever the quality of an education system and its schools at a given point in time, we shall strive to improve them, in the knowledge that perfection lies just around the corner. That is the human condition. That is the international imperative. That is the restless school.

As F. Scott Fitzgerald concludes of his great creation Jay Gatsby:

Gatsby believed in the green light, the orgiastic future that year by year recedes before us. It eluded us then, but that's no matter – tomorrow we will run faster, stretch out our arms farther….And one fine morning –

Roy Blatchford. Oxford & Geneva 2014

Chapter 2

A common purpose

Sir Thomas More: Why not be a teacher? You'd be a fine teacher; perhaps a great one.

Richard Rich: If I was, who would know it?

Sir Thomas More: You, your pupils, your friends, God. Not a bad public, that.

A Man for all Seasons, Robert Bolt

Winston Churchill memorably observed that in a maiden speech in Parliament, the Honorary Member should make no more than two main points, lest his audience forget the first.

In a spirit of 'less is more', I'm going to risk just three dangerous ideas in this 'common purpose' chapter.

First, that over the next decade, there must be a united and unashamedly positive approach to what our publicly-funded schools' system in the UK can deliver for children and young people.

Second, that some orthodoxies about *how* we deliver publicly funded education must be challenged.

Third, that school teaching, just somehow, must strive to become a profession.

The positive approach

You will probably know that the fifth most populous country in the world, if they all lived in the same place, is the 250 million international migrants who live in a country that they were not born in. So: China, India, the US, Indonesia, and then this extraordinary, contemporary diaspora.

The UK population is set to rise by 10 million over the next 25 years absorbing many of those international migrants.

120,000 more babies were born in this country in 2011, than in 2004.

An annual cohort of children entering the school system in 2020 will be 740,000; the current Year 11 is around 600,000.

If the UK stays intact, it will be the largest economy in Europe by 2025.

We must embrace this multi-cultural growth with all the wisdom of our islands' history. A 2013 report in *The Economist* highlighted that we are doing particularly well by many ethnic minorities, certainly when compared with their counterparts in other European countries.

At the same time we must borrow some of the *can-do* culture from other societies. The efficacy of a public service depends on an ethic of public service: profession as vocation. We must not run ourselves down, nor tolerate unchallenged those often misleading international comparisons on students' attainment. Benchmarked against the best yes, we must celebrate what we do well, constantly and loudly.

I worked for a period last year with some of the world's best international schools in the United Arab Emirates (UAE). One weekend I attended the UAE air show at which *196 billion dollars* worth of orders for new Boeing planes were placed, as part of their 2080 vision titled 'Beyond Oil'. Orders of stunning, forward-looking magnitude.

The ruler of Dubai, Sheikh Mohammed bin Rashid Al Maktoum's latest book *Flashes of Thought* contains these compellingly optimistic words:

'We, as leadership, seek happiness of our people in all areas and regions of the state. Start your day with positivity and optimism and with confidence in your abilities, and it will be reflected in your face, in your smile, in your interactions with people around you, and in the way you deal with daily challenges.'

And, significantly, this Sheikh has created, not the Department for Education, but *KHDA*: the Knowledge and Human Development Agency to oversee all public and private schools in the emirate.

Elsewhere in the UAE, one Education Council's ambitions for 2030 read: 'To produce world-class learners who embody a strong sense of culture and heritage and are prepared to meet global challenges'. Such countries are of course able to fix a clarity of mission without some of the messiness of the Western democracies. They are busy constructing 21st century nationhood without the complex historical baggage of an Industrial Revolution, Empire, and two World Wars. They are promoting themselves to business and future leaders through extensive global advertising.

What is also clear is that their leaders are seeking to bring into thoughtful balance key aspects of what is recognised globally as the Legatum Prosperity Index. Thus, education policy is not seen as separate from that which shapes social capital, entrepreneurship, health, security and governance. Short-termism may be the very stuff of Western politics. But it is no longer fit for purpose to address the challenges these nations face: providing good care for the elderly; containing drugs bills; developing sustainable housing and transport; funding primary, secondary and tertiary education.

Having lived in the western democracies for six decades, punctuated by periods of international travel and work, I am beginning to think that benign autocracies have something to teach us about positive vision, delivery and yes happiness and democracy for the citizen - I use the word citizen deliberately.

An effective, publicly-funded service requires a non-partisan ethic, and as a society in the UK we need to grasp this important reality if we wish to sit at the international high-table. Running our education system down, as happens all too frequently in the media and in our parliament too, is, like jealousy, corrosive of the spirit. It saps parental good-will from the system, it deters the best minds from becoming teachers, it acts as a negative force upon those who teach in and lead our schools.

Challenging orthodoxies

I grew up as a teacher in the Inner London Education Authority of the early 1970s, led by the visionary Peter Newsam, whom I note still writes trenchant letters to *The Times*. In that era, from Yorkshire to Devon, Local Education Authorities (LEA seems already a distant acronym) delivered a national service, for a local population. From the 1990s onwards, politicians of all parties have sought to challenge – on behalf of the voters – the monopoly state provision of a range of public services, from transport and housing to utilities and health. In education, academies and free schools are the most recent manifestation. Grant maintained status was an earlier version, and parent-sponsored academies may be a future iteration.

Thus we appear to have in England an inexorable march towards 25,000 independent state schools.

It is within these independent state schools, funded by the public purse, that we might challenge a few orthodoxies. I'll mention four here, which presage some futures thinking developed in Chapter 13.

1. We need to set new contracts for teachers which include an additional 10 to 15 days a year of high quality professional development – and a few academies and free schools have done this. We are all familiar with the oft-quoted mantra that no school system can be better than the quality of its teachers. Certainly, recruiting the brightest and best into teaching is a critical imperative in all nations, whatever their wealth or poverty.

2. We need, seriously, to enable teachers to teach until they are 70 by affording them sabbaticals and the chance to move, perhaps for short contracts, to areas of the country where school improvement needs are greatest. Personal and professional refreshment in a demanding role is vital if we are to meet the challenge of rising pupil numbers *and* retain our brightest and best. And the so-called PIT – the pool of inactive teachers – has to be reactivated and re-energised; there are too many well qualified and very competent teachers not plying their craft in classrooms.

3. We need to ensure that school buildings are used day-round and year-round to cater for the growth in pupil population. I have seen this first-hand in Egypt, Dubai, California and different parts of India.

To take one example from a London borough in 2013: 2000 pupils moved from its Year 6 to Year 7, while 3000 pupils arrived in that borough's Reception classes. What a challenge! And one which will unfold elsewhere in the country faster than we might imagine. The extraordinary becomes the commonplace, at a faster and faster rate. Communities must work together to overcome apparent obstacles to this kind of year-round schooling, and embrace an inevitable future.

4. We need a common inspection framework for state and independent schools in this country, as parts of the UAE have in successful operation. I have failed repeatedly to persuade Ministers of various political colours of the merits of an inspection system which would treat equally the great, state-funded Slough & Eton College and the great, privately-funded Eton College, barely a mile apart either side of the M4 motorway and with good views of Windsor Castle.

If you talk to both headteachers of these schools, you at once appreciate so much that they have in common. For their different school populations, they have a shared and palpable passion for developing students' leadership skills, resilience in the face of failure, and ambition for personal and others' successes.

How *does* school teaching ever become a profession?

In April 2014 I made a programme for BBC Radio 4 to mark 70 years since the 1944 Education Act (see page 143). What struck me in researching the programme – and having been in schools as pupil or teacher through most of those years – is the relentless to-fro futility acted out between successive governments and teachers, really since the late sixties. What all have demonstrated, sadly, is a manifest lack of common purpose.

Perhaps Aneurin Bevan should have stuffed teachers' mouths with gold in 1948 as he was alleged to have done with the doctors.

No matter now. Teachers and school leaders are well paid, and in many parts of the country today they are, as readers know, amongst the highest paid in their local communities.

I have played my own modest part to raise the status of teaching in co-authoring the 2012 Teachers' Standards, with its Preamble modelled on similar ones to be found in the medical and legal professions. This foundation statement reads:

Teachers make the education of their pupils their first concern, and are accountable for achieving the highest possible standards in work and conduct. Teachers act with honesty and integrity; have strong subject knowledge, keep their knowledge and skills as teachers up-to-date and are self-critical; forge positive professional relationships; and work with parents in the best interests of their pupils. (DfE 2012)

Over the past decade around the world I have observed close on 10,000 lessons in schools. In many classrooms, but not yet most, I experience teachers leading scholarship, ambition, intellectual curiosity and digression, the fun and fundamentals of that great double act which is teaching and learning.

Yet a child's unmet, unrequited thirst for knowledge – the hallmark of dull classrooms – is a feature I see too often in this and other countries.

In a recent study of how teachers are viewed around the world, researchers in different countries posed a simple question to diverse audiences: When I say the word 'teacher' to you, what other job do you think is the equivalent? In Japan, the most common response was 'local government manager'; in Germany it was 'social worker'; in the US it was 'librarian'; in China it was 'doctor'.

Librarians matter. Doctors matter. Teachers matter. Think of the great teachers you remember from your own school and university days. You won't remember them first and foremost for the quality of their marking (though I do remember well the spirited red ink of my fine A level English teacher), their report writing, or their ability to use the whiteboard if one existed. But you will always remember them with great affection and admiration because they remained young at heart – great teachers do. They made you feel valued as an individual, they treated you with dignity, they made you believe in yourself – in essence, they enabled you to be the confident adult now reading this book.

Thus I call for a united, positive, ambitious and learned approach – critically, with no-strike agreements as an essential public service – to be the cornerstone of a UK teaching profession, a profession which eludes us still.

Which returns me to my starting point of positive vision and delivery.

A common purpose

I worked enjoyably with Secretary of State for Education David Blunkett MP during the 1998 Year of Reading, and it felt like a year of common purpose in the many settings and schools we visited.

When governments help shape the best education service, they equip young people to build their future and so achieve happiness for themselves.

Let us seek to shape a common purpose in our schooling system, and not react unthinkingly to labels on schools' signs: state, independent, grammar, public, private, boarding, day, free, academy, and the rest. Given the history of education in England, these labels, if we allow, continue to create a divided education system. Dig deeper and what all schools have in common is their service to children and young people.

I repeat: an effective public service is rooted in an ethic of public service. That ethic needs to be championed by politicians and practitioners if a high quality education service is to be a hallmark of UK Ltd. in the coming decades.

Chapter 3

The Restless School

Some will say that we should not do anything in a class to encourage competition of any kind. To me this is foolish and unrealistic. Children are naturally and healthily competitive. They are interested in knowing who does things best, and they are all deeply interested in doing whatever they do today a little better than they did it yesterday. What is wrong with most schools is that we honour only a very few skills out of the great many that children possess.

How Children Fail, John Holt

'Someone's doing something special here'

Schools have marched a long way forward since John Holt's seminal book ignited a firestorm of controversy in the US in the mid-sixties.

I have had the privilege to visit a number of excellent schools – that is, schools which, as an inspector applying a particular framework and set of criteria in a particular jurisdiction, I have judged to be 'excellent' or 'outstanding'. There are in fact just a few schools internationally which for me 'stand out': groups of students, learning environments and teams of teachers coming together which you want to bottle and tell the educational world about. Dubai International Academy might be one; The Bridge School in Islington, London another; Shishuvan in Mumbai a third.

So what is the purposeful chemistry when I enter successfully run, very good schools which enjoy parental and student confidence, in the UK and globally?

- All around the school there are places of interest, challenge, wonder and reflection.

- The student voice is listened to and acted upon.

- The staff is committed to excellent teaching and an orderly, enthusiastic community.

- The leadership of the school promotes an aspirational culture – one of belief that children and young people can achieve more than they might have thought.

- Governors, parents and local people hold the school in high regard, and are involved in productive discourse about its vision and performance.

- Certain aspects stand out from the norm, both to those who work in the school, and to visitors who observe: 'Someone's doing something special here'.

Importantly, leaders know that it is not enough to get the ideas right; they have to be adopted. It is not enough to adopt the ideas; they have to be implemented correctly. And it is not enough to implement them correctly; they have to be constantly reviewed and adjusted over time as leaders see what works and what doesn't. The late Steve Jobs proclaimed a similar mantra at Apple, encouraging his workforce to 'fail wisely' in developing new products.

Restless to improve

Successful schools and their leaders are *restless*. There is a strange paradox at their core: they are very secure in their systems, values and successes yet simultaneously seeking to change and improve. These schools look inwards to secure wise development; they look outwards to seize innovation which they can hew to their own ends and, importantly, make a difference to the children and students they serve.

We *are* all deeply interested in doing better tomorrow what we did today. The most successful schools I know are *restless* to get better. They simply aren't content to stand still. So how do they do this?

First, they interrogate current routines; they confront comfortable orthodoxies; they challenge why they do what they do, from minor practical details to major policies.

Second, they harness a wide range of carefully gathered data, qualitative and quantitative; they know what pupils, staff, parents, governors, the wider community identify as strengths and relative weaknesses.

Third, they respond with timely, small-scale innovation pinpointed on a clear aspect for development. Committed 'can do' innovators on the staff show that a hitherto intractable problem can be solved, thoughtfully, and at the right pace for the school community.

Fourth, the small-scale innovation wins the hearts and minds of others. Gradually, whole-scale innovation takes root. Experiences and outcomes for pupils and staff are enriched.

Fifth – and to complete the virtuous circle – the school has now moved to a higher operational level; it is in a position to interrogate its routines from a better place.

In summary, a *knowledge base* is established; *innovation* is carefully introduced; *generalisation* about what works is understood and implemented, entering the bloodstream of the school. Restless schools – primary, special, secondary, all-through – are the ones which flourish. Reviewing and adjusting over time is the key to reinvigorating any business. Otherwise, stagnation beckons.

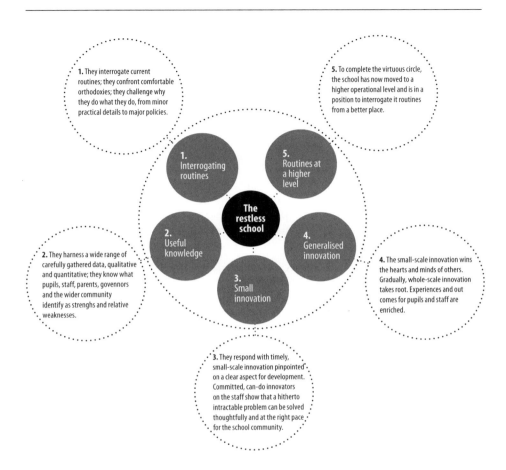

Key attributes

Digging beneath the surface of the restless school questing for excellence, unsurprisingly there is a lot going on, though the staff may not be shouting about it – they are happily focused. What are these key attributes?

Instantly palpable and visible is a pervading sense of the fun and fundamentals of learning: in classrooms, music and art studios, corridors, libraries, gymnasia and in the various outdoor learning environments. The teachers know about scholarship and creativity and talk openly about these vital ingredients in youngsters' enjoyment of school.

Day in and day out, restless schools accept no substitute for an evidence-based approach to what is happening in classrooms. Senior staff are not able to engage in anecdotal talk about, say, the under-performing science co-ordinator or Head of Design, because the senior team has clear and systematic evidence, rooted in regular lesson observations and teachers' own self-evaluations, on how all staff are performing in classrooms. Teachers are proud to teach with 'open doors'.

These schools build in rich opportunities for staff to conduct meaningful action research, and to apply the findings as appropriate. Teachers may well be pursuing Master's level and other courses of study.

In these thriving contexts, school leaders place great store by how well they create 'a sense of urgency at the right time' and a shared 'it's never too late' mentality amongst all staff. Confident, thoughtful and convincing headteachers recognise that not everything can be achieved at the same time, but that staff can 'shift gear' for a sustained period of time if there is that collective ambition to improve the school. Leaders at all levels believe that if change is worth introducing, why wait until a convenient point in the calendar, say the start of the following term? If pupils' experiences can be improved sooner, then the school should change its practices without delay. This is not a recipe for undue haste, but for accelerating change when change is required.

Equally, senior leaders and governors believe strongly in a 'no surprises' culture, and thus the importance of well-embedded systems that alert staff if pupils are at risk of under-achieving. Complementing the finely tuned organizational systems across the school is an open, trusting culture, one within which staff know that success is applauded, and failure is supported rather than invites blame.

In addition, leaders are very focused on eliminating 'in-school variation', or at least reaching a point where this had been reduced to an absolute minimum. One headteacher still striving for the school to be judged 'outstanding' made his mantra for the academic year: 'Let's all have a good year at the same time'.

Headteachers insist that timely communication of the highest quality, modelled by senior leaders, is at the heart of a high-performing institution. Such communication is always anticipating staff's and students' interests and concerns, so that the school is not side-tracked by rumour, gossip and unnecessary anxiety. Leaders know how to filter out external distractions, whether local politics or media hand-wringing about 'falling standards in schools'.

There is too an unequivocal sense that a 'we' not 'I' culture prevails – always beware of the headteacher who talks about '*my*' school! Leaders set out genuinely to see the best in people and dwell on the positive, while at the same time being single-minded in rooting out mediocrity.

And the voices of the students are not only heard but form an integral part of the development of the school. Their analysis and commentary upon all aspects of school provision – from classrooms and corridors to study and dining facilities – are woven into whole-school self-evaluation and forward planning. Students plan and lead activities and clubs for fellow students.

Those charged with the responsibility of governance consider that an excellent school is one in which *everyone* feels they are making a contribution. In personal and professional terms, all students and staff believe and know they have a 'next step' to make within the institution, and that the institution supports, values and celebrates those next steps. The most effective governing bodies and school boards believe their role is to intervene if required, but principally to ensure that the senior leadership team and staff do not digress from their core activities.

Harnessing inspection

From inspecting schools in different parts of the world, applying bespoke and contextually specific inspection frameworks, I recognise common and altogether appropriate responses by school leaders.

When schools receive a 'good' inspection, they decide that to achieve 'excellent' or 'outstanding' is a natural next step. Senior leaders ask all staff to read the reports of schools which have been judged 'outstanding'. Staff then commit themselves to ensuring that the same kind of phrases they have been reading in 'excellent' reports can, in time, be readily written about their own school.

Schools place great emphasis on everyone on the staff knowing and understanding the language of the inspection framework. In-service sessions are focused on all teaching and support staff securing a strong grasp of the difference between 'good' and 'outstanding', whether in relation to teaching, assessment, pupils' independent learning, or leadership at all levels?

Further, senior leaders in schools try to 'climb inside the inspector's skin'. Leaders seek to share with all staff *how* the inspection process works, enabling staff to see the school from the 'outside in'.

Schools on the journey from good to great use their self-evaluation documentation as a key driver with all staff. Different teams and groups of staff are asked to focus on different aspects of their Self-Evaluation Schedule, reviewing which aspects of the school's practice and impact on students need to improve so that grade boundaries in the inspection framework are crossed, from grade two to grade one.

Brighton Rock

There are, in my view, three further and telling characteristics of the restless school. Like Brighton though the proverbial stick of rock, snap open the restless school, and you will see the following.

- *Great schools cite the value of 'external critical friends'.* These reviewers are invited on a regular basis to see the school with a fresh pair of eyes – but not too often, less their fresh eyesight dims. These eyes validate changes, champion best practice and point out, without fear or favour, where there is headroom for further improvement. Importantly, this external view strengthens leaders' capacity to articulate clearly the objectives of the school - and the benefits of being part of its community - alongside some grounded and externally validated assessment of both its performance and future plans.

- *The best schools 'tighten up' to be good, but 'loosen' to become outstanding.* They recognise the importance of high levels of quality control to secure good provision, evolving into higher levels of quality assurance. Thus a whole-school culture of excellence is created, within which teachers and students feel empowered to take measured risks.

Schools are fundamentally about what occurs in classrooms. Liberating teachers to be 'maverick' in the best sense of the word is crucial. It is the accomplished, freed teacher, comfortable in her own knowledge of subject matter, who is able to master and manage high quality digression, without fear of criticism of being 'off syllabus'. To watch creative intellectual digression which builds on pupils' previous knowledge and dares them to think differently – whether in the early years' outdoor learning area or in an A level economics seminar – is to witness fine learning.

- *The successful, restless school is thoughtfully 'outward-facing'.* Significant numbers of staff work on external agendas, sometimes linked to training school status; sometimes to 'statistical neighbours' in examination performance; sometimes to soft and hard federations and primary-secondary clusters; sometimes to international partners. These schools enjoy partnerships with other schools and education providers: their staff are constantly bringing back strong practices into their own classrooms from external sources. Staff then blend home-grown practice and resources with those they have cherry-picked from elsewhere. In turn, reaching out generously to support other schools is in their life-blood.

Leaders know intuitively that innovation can come from without as well as from within. To borrow again from the iconic Steve Jobs in his pomp, the real skill lies in stitching together a school's own ideas with those from outside and then wrapping the results in 'elegant software and stylish design'. There is no such thing as a copyright on ideas.

Leadership in a global setting

And I'll tell it and speak it and think it and breathe it
And reflect from the mountain so all souls can see it

Bob Dylan's 1963 song *A Hard Rain's Gonna Fall* has often served to remind me that leadership is about telling compelling stories which others believe and follow. The convincing leadership of schools around the world today, state or independent, seems to me rooted in the following five dimensions, which leaders in different places and different contexts weigh as more or less important.

Leaders:

- Believe in the joy of learning and the moral purpose of education
- Strive to raise student achievement and broaden opportunities
- Explore and harness the different ways in which students and staff learn, in and outside of classrooms
- Share roles and responsibilities widely within the school
- Shape vibrant partnerships and promote school-to-school support.

Further, effective school leaders hold onto what religious and non-religious elders alike have long taught: without a vision the people perish. Leaders recognise they have to know their song well before they start singing. They know they have to set out and reinforce constantly, through the spoken and written word, that vision for their own school community.

Leaders know too that without a vision properly communicated, confusion reigns.

A short story to conclude. The setting is a hierarchical secondary school of 2000 students where morning prayers by Tannoy were once the norm. I was there.

A cautionary tale

Head to Deputy: Tomorrow morning there will be an eclipse of the sun at 9am. This is something we can't see every day. Let the pupils line up outside in their best clothes to watch. To mark the occurrence of this rare phenomenon I will personally explain it to them. If it is raining we shall not be able to see it very well and so the pupils should assemble in the hall.

Deputy Head to Senior Teacher: By order of the Head there will be a total eclipse of the sun at 9am tomorrow. If it is raining we shall not be able to see very well on sight, in our best clothes. In that case the disappearance of the sun will be followed through in the hall. This is something that we can't see happen every day.

Senior Teacher to Head of Year: By order of the head we shall follow through, in best clothes, the disappearance of the sun in the hall tomorrow morning at 9am. The Head will tell us whether it is going to rain. This is something we can't see happen every day.

Head of Year to Form Tutor: If it is raining in the hall tomorrow morning, which is something we can't see happen every day, the Head – in her best clothes – will disappear at 9am.

Form Tutor to Pupils: Tomorrow at 9am the Head will disappear. It is a pity that we cannot see this happen every day.

Chapter 4

Values added

Any teacher who smokes, uses liquor in any form, frequents pool or public halls, or gets shaved in a barber shop will give good reason to suspect his worth, intention, integrity and honesty.

Rules for Teachers 1872

Unchanging values of schools

Why abandon a belief
Merely because it ceases to be true.
Cling to it for long enough, and not a doubt
It will turn true again, for so it goes.
Most of the change we think we see in life
Is due to truths being in and out of favour.
As I sit here, and often times, I wish
I could be monarch of a desert land
I could devote and dedicate forever
To the truths we keep coming back and back to.

'The Black Cottage' by Robert Frost

In other words, if you stand still long enough, you become a radical. Or as I once heard the same sentiment put succinctly in a headteacher's retirement speech: 'I've been head here for 25 years, and have been at the cutting edge three times.'

Reflecting for a few moments on Robert Frost's lines above, what are the truths I keep coming back to in relation to my working in and with schools?

First, we know that schools matter, that the provision of a well-ordered, stimulating learning environment is a common right for all our children. Truly, each child has one chance. That was profoundly reinforced for me during the many visits I made, as one of Her Majesty's Inspectors in England, to schools where provision was inadequate in all kinds of ways; and of course the pupils knew no different, even though many of the teachers and leaders did.

Second, we know that schools matter more and more as the traditional family unit is less constant for many children. Whatever else they do, schools need to define, refine and articulate social and moral values and respect for others, irrespective of their class, sex, race, religion or heritage tongue. That was as true for me as a young teacher in multi-racial Brixton in 1973, as it was in 1986 when I took up a secondary headship in a largely mono-cultural Oxfordshire, as it is today throughout our pluralist and diverse kingdom.

Third, we believe, do we not, that schools must promote the highest achievement in youngsters, *irrespective* of their abilities or self-expectations. Students' various aspirations should be harnessed. Competition and collaboration must play equally in learning.

Fourth, we celebrate, in a climate of equal opportunity and access to that opportunity, a broad range of achievements. We challenge fixed notions of ability. We value and reward children's oral, practical, academic, sporting, artistic and yes, leadership skills. Howard Gardner's writings on multiple intelligences have influenced successive generations of teachers in this field.

Fifth, we believe that an effective and flourishing school should be 'public' rather than 'private', explaining to parents and families what is being taught and how the curriculum is being interpreted. It should be open to praise and criticism (not blame) in a genuine spirit of partnership, while at the same time reasonably affirming that judgements about pedagogy rest with the professionals. We don't go to the hospital with a broken leg and start advising the surgeon where and how to insert the stabilising pins.

Those are the five truths which, taking Robert Frost's words in *The Black Cottage*, I 'keep coming back and back to'. Those are the truths which have guided me through 40 years of teaching and headship, and currently inform all my work with schools at home and abroad. In turn, they have led me to believe and advocate with schools across the world that it is *values added* which are of profound importance in schooling.

You will have your own precious truths and deeply held values which guide you. Pause ... and you might reflect for just a moment on what they are.

***

Schools are crucibles of values; indeed they provide oases of calm and stability for those children who perhaps lead otherwise chaotic and fractured lives. Yes, schools remain places and agents of social control. In how time is orchestrated, they are remarkably unchanged, particularly primary schools. I warmly say about most primaries in 2014 that they are as Bathwick Primary School, Bath was for me in 1957 – reading, writing and arithmetic in the morning, and nature study after lunch. We may call it phonics, number bonds and design and technology today, but the flow remains the same ... and why not?

Look back in the log-books of 19th century primary schools, and what shines though the copper-plate text is that preoccupation with pupils' attendance and behaviour. Read into the log-book pages of the early 20th century, and payment by results looms large.

With secondary schools, it's the tyranny of the timetable all day that remains unchanged. There are some notable exceptions, most often to be found in independent schools.

There is a deeply conservative strand in our schools as agents of the state – and we are not alone across the globe. Someone has to look after children and young people during daylight hours. Opening up a new school and learning centre in Milton Keynes at the start of this century I was able to persuade parents and the local community that 16 year-olds could have a study afternoon at home once a week. Proposing similar at the time to a conference of secondary headteachers in the West Midlands, the first challenge I encountered was: 'And what did the police say?'

Equally, let it be said proudly that schools embody continuity, tradition, constancy in a changing world. Schools in any culture seek to balance the transmission of values from the past with anticipation of future cultural norms. We forget this at our individual and collective peril. The architect Richard Rogers argues compellingly: 'Architecture is measured against the past, you build in the present and you try to imagine the future'. So too with schools. Through the common eye, schools are immutably of the past, the present and the future.

If you want a warm and bewitching account of life unchanging, or maybe changing ever so slowly, read the following – carefully and deliberately. It is the full, unpublished, two-paragraph report by one of Her Majesty's Inspectors of Schools in England. The setting is Norfolk.

BEACHAMWELL COUNTY FIRST SCHOOL

HM Miss F E Ball

NOR 21

Beachamwell lies in that quiet triangle made by Swaffham, Downham and Mundford and neighbours, in a nudging kind of way, the villages of Cockley Cley and Barton Bendish. The flatness of Swaffham Heath, once a tangled mass of stunted alders, scrub oak and grunting of wild pigs, is now a mixture of arable, conifer and mixed deciduous woodland. Barley whispers to itself in the cold wet wind but the pheasants, fat and arrogant as turkeys, scratch around in the sugar beet as if they were farmyard fowls. There is no gamekeeper to keep the jay in check and the Magpie flaunts his neat black and white outfit with the careless rapture of the sober middle-aged suddenly drunk with the joy of living. In the village the silence is that of the deep country, a bird sings, the wind is rebuked by the swaying trees, an aeroplane grumbles past, out of sight well above the low cloud. The church clothed in the peace of centuries sits and waits with its thatched roof and fretted round tower closer to time long gone than the tractored, horseless age that now enfolds it.

Miss Ball, who came as head teacher in October 1976 from the United Nations School in Switzerland, appears to have made this small school come alive. Much of the children's work is on display and even in the art work it is obvious that they are being encouraged to observe carefully.

There is the right emphasis on skills and the enthusiasm of the Head is reflected in the adoration seen in the eyes of the young children. Already these children have been taken on a theatre visit to Norwich and two further visits are planned. Miss Ball has part-time assistance – a.m. only – but this teacher was not seen. Miss Ball said that she was given an assurance on appointment that the school would remain open for some years. The school building remains the same as mentioned in Mr Symonds' note of last visit but Miss Ball has managed to wheedle new furniture and a variety of extras from the LEA. There can be little doubt that she is the best thing to happen to Beachamwell since they stopped burning their witches.

W. H. Thompson 15 June 1977

Classroom values

The classroom: the place where, for up to 190 days a year, teachers and children and young people spend six, seven or eight hours together. What *are* the underlying values that inform these vital environments? Influenced by the thinking of a number of colleagues, I suggest that they fall into the following three categories.

First, there are moral and even perhaps spiritual values.

Education aims to achieve central moral purposes: it is in essence about helping people to grow into autonomous, morally-literate human beings who become valued members of society and citizens. There is, of course, plenty of room for debate about how best it does this, and what are the central features of a morally-educated person. But what is surely incontestable is that not only *what* we teach but *how* we teach can make a great difference to our students: whether by precept, example or demeanour, teachers exert a moral influence, for better or worse.

A former HMI colleague of mine regularly quotes the religious education teacher who went round the class saying, 'Remember, God is Love' while vigorously striking the pupils on the head with a Bible.

Successful pedagogy is informed by positive human qualities such as sensitivity, concern for individuals, compassion and kindness. It is also imbued with a desire to cultivate in one's students such educational outcomes as moral responsibility, spiritual awareness, socially-cohesive attitudes, respect for cultural diversity, an understanding of right and wrong.

No doubt there are some who will think to themselves: 'how is any of this going to help them to get through geography GCSE?' But think about it. In a nutshell, the teacher who is passionate, humane, civilised, scholarly and also excited about the subject and subject-matter is also the teacher whose students do best in tests and examinations.

Second, any selection of teaching methods or learning approaches makes its own value assumptions and by implication transmits these.

It is easy to see this if one studies how the aim of unquestioned or unquestioning religious, ideological or political indoctrination is best achieved through certain highly structured and authoritarian teaching methods, including a heavy dose of rote learning. Open questions would plainly be counter-productive.

Conversely, learning by enquiry or research is likely to imply a commitment to following truth wherever it may be found, to basing actions on evidence and exploration, to a willingness to doubt, test and evaluate independently. Use of practical methods is based on a recognition that often we learn best by doing – an old truth, but often a true one. Encouragement of wide reading and research presupposes the values of intellectual curiosity, open-ended enquiry, and the subjecting of ideas or hypotheses to a variety of views and interpretations in order to arrive at a well-grounded conclusion.

Third, the whole way in which learning is organised and managed rests on fundamental educational beliefs about the learner and the learning process.

It is for this reason, in effect, that inspectors and lesson observers bang on endlessly about *differentiation*.

It is not just that doing things differently for different people relieves tedium and is more efficient as a means of instruction. Above all, it is the fact that the key moral value – however difficult to uphold consistently – is that each member of the class is an individual with her or his own rights, character, disposition to learning and level of understanding.

It therefore follows that any teaching which short-changes any one individual is a failure to apply the core moral principles of equity and human rights, since it privileges one learner over another, one form of ability over another.

Society, childhood and adolescence

Perhaps we have Shakespeare to hold to account for a rather withering view of adolescence:

'I would there was no age between sixteen and three-and-twenty, or that youth would sleep out the rest; for there is nothing in the between but getting wenches with child, wronging the ancientry, stealing and fighting'.

The Winter's Tale. William Shakespeare

No less an authority than best-selling children's author Jacqueline Wilson has written of how deeply concerned she is that children are growing up too fast. As a fan of her writing and one who reviewed for the education press a number of her early novels, I observe that she has spent a career writing about divorce and single motherhood, and has championed teenage characters (who can forget Tracy Beaker on page or screen?) who are precocious, worldly-wise, and wear dazzling make-up and hip-hugging jeans. Is she reflecting teenagers or are they aspiring to her fictional image of them?

Local and national politicians of every hue continue the clarion call: rarely does a month pass by without a party spokesperson denouncing some aspect of Britain's toxic childhood, whether knife-carrying, manifesting delinquent behaviour in shopping malls, or indulging in binge drinking – 'wronging the ancientry' indeed.

It is certainly true that there are social pressures on most youngsters to achieve, behave and consume like adults at an earlier and earlier age. Yes, mental health concerns are real and a small minority of young people sadly do experience abused lives. But as someone who every week is with pupils in classrooms, corridors and canteens, I wish to present an alternative prospectus.

Almost every child I speak with testifies to how safe and secure they feel in the school environment, well supported by their teachers. Canteen menus and lunch-boxes reveal a keen awareness amongst students of healthy eating, happily at odds with much press stereotyping.

The overwhelming majority of young people speak highly of their enjoyment of lessons and especially of extracurricular activities. Schools are places of purposeful fun and natural laughter which no adult office environment I have encountered can begin to match. From an early age, many youngsters are engaged in buddying schemes, charity fund-raising, and volunteering both within school and extending generously into their local communities.

The vast majority of youngsters feel positive about themselves because teachers are dedicated to raising their self-esteem, being as focused on *values added* as on measurable *value-added*, to use the jargon of assessment. Young people in schools and classrooms around the world today articulate values of genuine altruism, treat one another with dignity, and are proud to be young citizens of the globe. In so many ways, they see themselves as social entrepreneurs.

Paul Collier's seminal book *The Bottom Billion* is a contemporary clarion call for forthcoming generations to end the grinding poverty and starvation of one sixth of humankind. Away from the media gaze and reactive political rhetoric, I know that the current generation in our schools and colleges are of a mindset and predisposition to address this call. Their values matter profoundly to them.

Chapter 5

Value added

We are going to die, and that makes us the lucky ones. Most people are never going to die because they are never going to be born. The potential people who could have been here in my place but who will in fact never see the light of day outnumber the sand grains of Arabia. Certainly those unborn ghosts include greater poets than Keats, scientists greater than Newton. We know this because the set of possible people allowed by our DNA so massively exceeds the set of actual people. In the teeth of these stupefying odds it is you and I, in our ordinariness, that are here.

Unweaving the Rainbow, Richard Dawkins

Slack

Through watching the indomitable Olympic athlete Mo Farah, I have been introduced to the world of Alberto Salazar.

Salazar won the New York marathon three consecutive times, and was rated as the greatest distance runner in the world for the first half of the 1980s. Then he turned to coaching others, specialising in high-altitude training in Utah, including Mo Farah.

Early in the summer of 2007 Salazar began feeling a pain in his neck. He was having a heart attack. His face turned purple. He had no pulse. Blood trickled out of his mouth. His brain was without oxygen for twelve minutes. Finally, his heart fluttered back to life, courtesy of an energetic defibrillator. He wrote later: 'None of the doctors who treated me, and none of the experts I've consulted since the day I collapsed, have ever heard of anybody being gone for that long and coming back to full health.'

Salazar was back coaching on the track nine days after the attack. Now Salazar is clearly no slouch: in the context of running and life, he had a passion and self-belief that he would not be beaten. Simply, he gave of his utmost best all of the time, driven by some intangible inner demon.

Maybe this is a sporting thing. David Brailsford, leader of British Cycling, pronounced immediately after the 2012 Olympics that in Rio de Janeiro in 2016 the Brits should seek out all ten golds, not just aim to repeat the seven won in London. 'Our job is to believe it is possible to do even better,' he said.

Brailsford went on to say: 'If we replicate what is going on in broader society, you have to make the expenditure you have more efficient. There is enough slack in our system to make it more efficient, and more streamlined and leaner.'

Is he right? Can we apply lessons from the intense cauldron of elite sport to other aspects of society, including the schools system? Can the Brailsford philosophy of *the science of marginal gains* be applied to the work of pupils and teachers?

The answer, in part at least, must be yes. But there are some provisos.

For most of us, slack – the gap between what is possible, under conditions of absolute effort, and actual performance – is unavoidable. An article on fine dining in Washington D.C. recorded that out of dozens of restaurants in that city which aspire to be first class, only five to ten really were top-notch at any given time. A restaurant can be great for its first three to six months, as the chefs and the owners strive to make the best possible impression on diners and reviewers. But once these places become popular, their obsession with quality slacks off – 'they become socialising scenes and their audiences become automatic.'

The political economist Albert Hirschman has explored this notion of slack in his fascinating book *Exit, Voice, and Loyalty,* the premise being that slack is part of what we take as normal and natural about the world. He writes in the opening chapter:

'Slack has somehow not only come into the world and exists in given amounts, but it is continuously being generated as a result of some sort of entropy characteristic of human, surplus-producing societies.' He argues that organisations are conceived to be permanently and randomly subject to decline and decay, to a gradual loss of efficiency and energy, no matter how well the institutional framework within which they function is designed.

We are not perfect. 'Perfected' humans lie in the science fiction pages of Huxley, Aldiss and Bradbury. In the end, it is the human condition for us to be slackers, accepting that the gap between what is possible and actual performance will nearly always exist, in any context from family relationships to the workplace.

If it's not a recipe for depressing expectations – and I certainly do not intend that – perhaps we should accept that it is only rare high performers who, for short bursts in their life, are able to attain outstanding feats? When they do, what excitement they bring! For the mortals amongst us, let us live content with a bit of slack.

I have elaborated on this subject of slack because, if we are not careful, a contemporary world in which there is a plethora of data can drive us to think that only the very best is worth achieving. Nothing else matters. Further, we risk falling victim to the so-called McNamara fallacy, a short text which is well worth reading slowly, with pauses:

'The first step is to measure whatever can be easily measured. This is OK as far as it goes. The second step is to disregard that which can't be easily measured or to give it an arbitrary quantitative value. This is artificial and misleading. The third step is to presume that what can't be measured easily really isn't important.

This is blindness. The fourth step is to say what can't be easily measured really doesn't exist. This is suicide.'

I have in the past – less so these more informed days – seen this approach to measurement applied in schools and colleges. Its logical simplicity can be dangerously seductive. Thus, a school can readily measure pupils' attendance or library borrowing rates or reading ages – fine. But what about resilience, self-esteem and happiness, all vital to a student's well-being and success? We need to think carefully about what is and is not possible to measure, and find ways to record and report meaningfully.

As an inspector over many years and in many jurisdictions I have regularly asked myself: Is this school better than its data? Can it be? Is it not as good as its data? On which aspects of provision does the school keep data? And which data are most important?

Assessment and value added

Assessment is an integral part of the teaching and learning process. It takes a variety of forms and interventions: oral checking of understanding in the commerce of the classroom; diagnosing misunderstandings and misconceptions; regular tests and intermittent examinations; marking students' work with diagnostic, formative and summative comments; discussion of 'next steps' and how to improve on previous skills or knowledge acquisition; teachers modelling a discreet skill to help move on the learner.

Assessment, for both pupil and teacher, looks a little different in a class of five year olds and in a class of 16-year-olds. Some use red pens, some use green, and some use portable devices. It takes on different guises if the subject is design or music or physical education or history. At root however, the straight-forward purposes are the same:

- to check progress
- to provide motivation
- to inform next steps in teaching.

Unquestionably, wise and timely feedback and intervention fuel progress, in any learning context. The sharper and more focused the feedback, the more useful for the student.

Assessment as described above is fundamentally active and about classroom process. Its timing, form and practice are best left to the professional judgement of teachers, working within an appropriate whole-school framework.

There are of course wider applications in the school system of the word 'assessment'. Importantly, assessment enables students, their families and their teachers to make decisions about education and training. Externally validated assessment provides an accurate and timely appraisal of achievement and capability, whether that is GCSE, IGCSE, NVQ, A level or IB.

Given the forensic focus there now is around the world on how each and every school performs, it is vital that teachers and leaders are in proper command of assessment, internal and external. Too much rides on this for it to be treated casually. How much *value* schools add is what inspection systems focus upon. What was the child's starting point? Three, five or seven years later, how much value has been added? How much progress have they made from a given starting point? The questions can, in the wrong hands, sound reductive of human achievement, but they are a contemporary reality.

It is salient to observe here that wise target setting in schools focuses on targets which are at one and the same time *plausible* and *challenging,* for pupils and teachers alike. Significant amounts of time are expended on target setting, at all levels in all school systems. Purpose, culture, process and presentation need to be got right if targets are to motivate not depress.

Echoing back to the McNamara fallacy, an education system should deliver what is important, rather than value just what can be most readily measured. If we are not careful, the amount of time spent on testing and examinations can distort teaching and learning, and be disproportionately time consuming.

As we look ahead, there is an inexorable drive – given the global data movement – to have similar or parallel testing and examination systems which allow comparisons of students' performance in different countries to be made; TIMSS and PISA come to mind. In my view, this will happen sooner than we think and as early as in primary education. As long as the public purse pays, governments on behalf of the electorate want to know that billions of pounds being invested in education are having the required impact.

A former HMI colleague of mine was once asked to explain the complexity of the English examination system to a group of visiting Principals from India. He left the room – to cry, and to compose himself, before re-entering. If we are not careful, school leaders can tie themselves in unwarranted knots worrying about our over-complicated and sometimes confusing array of tests, examinations, qualifications and their equivalents.

Yes, through various professional and media channels we should seek to shape and influence the national debate. But the pressing imperative week in and week out is to make the system work, for the benefit of children and students.

To take the higher ground, we must shape 'assessment' so that it:

    a.   serves pupils and teachers well every day in classrooms

    b.   serves pupils and families well in keeping them informed of progress on a regular basis

    c.   validates reliably the achievements of one student compared with another

    d.   enables proper decisions to be made about transition between one phase of education and the next

e. enables inspectors and government to make wise judgements about value- added and the effective use of public resources; or, in the case of privately funded schools, the effective use of fees.

Marginal gains

To return to David Brailsford and the science of marginal gains. Aside from his spectacular successes with the British cycling team, he has enjoyed further triumphs with Bradley Wiggins and Christopher Froome being consecutive Tour de France winners. About these victories he observes: 'People often associate marginal gains with pure technology, but it is far more than that. It is about nutrition, ergonomics, psychology. It is about making sure the riders get a good night's sleep by transporting their own bed and pillow to each hotel. It is about using the most effective massage gel. Each improvement may seem trivial, but the cumulative effect can be huge.'

Chapter 4 highlighted the importance of values added, and I have mentioned above the critical importance of students' well-being and self-esteem. How a child feels about him or herself on arriving at each lesson should matter to a school as much as beds and gels matter to Brailsford's cyclists.

With every school wanting to shape its own marginal gains in order to improve students' performance – to improve value added measures – leaders need to focus on specific ways in which aspects of assessment (in its broadest sense) can be sharpened. How can marking in English, science and mathematics books have just that greater impact on accelerating pupils' progress? How can the school improve the quality and timing of written reports so that parents can support their children at home more effectively? How can we prepare students just that little bit differently so they enter the examination room in a great frame of mind?

And when the occasion arises for a school to lay out its achievements to the passing inspector, how can leaders present pupils' progress and attainment data in a more accessible and focused format?

***

The quotation from Richard Dawkins, a self-professed atheist, at the start of this chapter reminds each one of us of our spectacular 'ordinariness'. Effective schools set out to build upon each child's unique ordinariness. These primary, special and secondary schools alike ensure that values added and value added weigh equally on the journey.

As a secondary headteacher in Oxfordshire for ten years I worked throughout that period with the same secretary. She and her husband had three children go up through the school; I taught them all. It was she who, to this day, reminds me that the best tribute she can make to the school was that it had – alongside her own fine parenting – produced three happy and open-minded young adults, ready to take on the world. Yes, they had each moved on from school to good universities. More importantly, they are today confident citizens and parents.

To conclude on matters of importance.

A story I'm fond of sharing with sixth-form students runs as follows. It's in the form of a letter by an 18 year-old girl away at boarding school writing to her parents.

Dear Mummy and Daddy

I have to tell you that I have ended up – unexpectedly – in hospital, with both legs broken. I have also fallen in love with an Australian nurse – in fact, we are going to get married, emigrate and I am about to have his baby.

None of the above is true, but I have just failed my final exams, and I thought you ought to put things in perspective!

Yours,
Trudy

Chapter 6

Does it matter what we teach?

Do not confine your children to your own learning, for they were born in another time.

Hebrew proverb

Shift happens

As the year 2000 approached, the publishing industry went into overdrive. Numerous books summarised human achievement in the 20th century and went on to make predictions for humankind as the new millennium was born. What would be the future megatrends to underpin our lives? Foremost amongst them were: a renaissance in the arts; global economic boom; the triumph of free-market socialism and cultural nationalism; the privatisation of the welfare state; the rise of the Pacific Rim; the triumph of the individual; religious revivalism. And, of course, the utopian quest for peace and prosperity for all.

Already into the second decade of the 21st century and we can see which of these has begun to surface as significant globally. On the one hand, making predictions is a mug's game. On the other it's fun, a natural and important aspect of being human.

The futurologist Richard Watson has identified five key trends in the world for the next fifty years: ageing; the power shift eastwards; global connectivity; the environment; and the GRIN technologies: genetics, robotics, internet and nanotechnology. Today, you would not bet against any of these being significant in the geopolitical thinking of governments across the world.

Turning those reflections towards the education of the young, what are the potential implications? Can we make just a few intelligent guesses?

A child born in the UK this year and entering school in 2018 will likely live well into the 22nd century; as health-care, nutrition and compulsory education spread across all societies, so will an increasing number of her global peers. She will certainly witness in her lifetime China and India overtaking the USA as the largest world economies, and all kinds of power shifts from West to East. She may or may not remain in the UK throughout adulthood, with the fastest growing 'country' in the world being that which currently comprises the 250 million people who live outside the country of their birth. There is no turning back on that global migration and immigration.

It is safe to assert that she will work in a society where downloading human intelligence into a machine is no longer the stuff of science fiction. That will be commonplace, and adding human consciousness to that machine will follow. She will watch as societies grow richer, and while great inequalities will remain, all signs are that extremes of poverty will gradually fall to an irreducible minimum. Most fundamentally, natural resources as we know them will have been exhausted or severely depleted and climate patterns will continue to evolve, often with terrifying impact on the world's peoples. There will have to be – for this girl born in 2014 and her peers – a profound shift in attitudes and human behaviours.

Curriculum implications

What does all this mean for a school and what course of study, formal and informal, it should teach the children?

As an idea, the word 'curriculum' came from the Latin meaning a race or the course of a race, and has over time come to be used as the catch-all word for all the learning which is planned and guided by the school – *a course of study*. 'Extracurricular' has always struck me as an odd word for schools to use about their after-school programmes, but has entered into common parlance; and a number of educational commentators have enjoyed exploring the so-called 'hidden curriculum'.

In the same way that schools in any society are immutably of the past, present and the future, what they choose to teach their children is a similar blend of history, contemporary knowledge, and a skills set for today and tomorrow.

The current political consensus in England is that while there is a prescribed National Curriculum, by becoming academies (independent state schools) 'freedom' from a centrally laid down curriculum can be secured. I wonder whether this freedom is misplaced. Politically, the mantra is about freeing up schools from state control. That's fine as far as it goes. But look around the world. From my school inspection and review experiences, whether in New York or Barcelona, Abu Dhabi or Bangkok, Jeddah or Mumbai, nations retain a firm grip on their respective national curricula. And it is still more or less the case in France today that when 13 year-old students in Toulouse open their geography books in January to study volcanoes, their peers in Lille are turning to the same pages!

Why do countries maintain this central direction? They are surely affirming that, through a commonly shared curriculum, they are passing on to the next generation the nation's history, traditions and values, as well as preparing their students for today's and tomorrow's global society with skills and knowledge the nation believes will be of value. For example, throughout the United Arab Emirates, all schools – government, independent, international – must teach Arabic and Islamic Studies to a good standard to all students, a proper affirmation of the cultural and religious importance of the two subjects in those emirates.

Countries across the world, regardless of their wealth or political complexion, are wrestling with similar themes and tensions around the purposes of education, and thus its content. In particular, they are debating:

- Knowledge versus process and skills – either/or?
- Securing the 3Rs
- Technology – opportunity or distraction?
- Education for creating civilised citizens or tomorrow's workforce – either/or?
- Education for global citizenship.

(For further background on this debate, see Deborah Eyre in *Taking forward the Primary Curriculum*, ed. Roy Blatchford)

Does it matter what we teach?

Interestingly, many respected research studies and educational commentators in recent years would say not. In McKinsey's influential studies 'How the world's best performing school systems come out on top' (2007) and its sequel 'How the world's most improved school systems keep getting better' (2010), the curriculum is not a key matter, certainly not in comparison with the quality of teachers and investment in their training.

Yet for me, memorable lessons are rooted in a rich curriculum, carefully planned and skilfully resourced by the teacher. In the best schools and the most engaging classrooms, teachers have a very clear idea of the social, personal and intellectual outcomes they wish pupils to achieve.

Teachers know well their individual pupils' predispositions to learn. They recognise which teaching and learning styles and curriculum content are more or less effective. Above all in a very good classroom, teachers have a clear grasp of the potential pupils have to develop their multiple intelligences, talents and aptitudes in various directions.

In great classrooms, there is not a single and simple curriculum blueprint. Schools and teachers follow different paths, and rightly so. But there is a clarity of vision and purpose about the planned curriculum. And the process of groups of teachers reviewing and creating their curriculum offer frequently leads to excellent teaching.

One further reflection on what we teach and why.

In a now celebrated speech in 1976 at Ruskin College (and one which led to the eventual introduction of a National Curriculum in England), Prime Minister James Callaghan set out to explore what he said had remained for too long in English schools, the 'secret garden' of the curriculum. Carefully harnessing the words of R.H Tawney – 'What a wise parent would wish for their children, so the state must wish for all its children' – Callaghan moved on to say:

The goals of our education, from nursery school through to adult education, are clear enough. They are to equip children to the best of their ability for a lively, constructive place in society, and also to fit them to do a job of work. Not one or the other but both.

There is a simplicity, clarity and inclusivity about these words that can serve curriculum planners to this day.

If we believe that schooling is merely about the training of the intellect, then schools will be narrowly focused and exam success will remain the Holy Grail. If we have a broader vision of what it means to be human – artistic faculties, sporting prowess, moral sensibilities, spiritual quest – then schools will strive to educate the whole child. What is not identified and nurtured by the age of 16, and usually long before, is likely to remain dormant for life.

And in the words of one sage, which those shaping innovative curricula might wish to fathom:

An ounce of information is worth a pound of data

An ounce of knowledge is worth a pound of information

An ounce of understanding is worth a pound of knowledge

An ounce of wisdom is worth a pound of understanding.

Primary curriculum

Primary schools I visit around the globe are invariably warm and welcoming places to be for children. Laughter, creativity and a sense of colour permeate corridors, hallways, playgrounds and classrooms. The vast majority of these schools know that a concentration on the basics of language, mathematics, sciences, the arts, humanities and physical education is an entitlement for all. How they design their curriculum, what topics they teach and in what order, whether they teach indoors or outdoors, what their approach is to meta-cognition, how they promote spirituality, how they assess and report on progress – these remain within a school's proper jurisdiction. What matters is that the day-to-day experience has a positive effect on growing and voracious minds.

One school may adopt the fast expanding International Primary Curriculum (*www.greatlearning.com/ipc*), which has distinct subject, personal and international goals, underpinned by specific knowledge, skills and understanding. The IPC unit themes include a smorgasbord of topics from the oil industry, climate, migration and astronomy, to current affairs, sustainability and relationships education.

Another school may root its curriculum in the learner profile set out in the very well established and trusted International Baccalaureate (*www.ibo.org*), seeking to produce learners who are inquirers, knowledgeable, thinkers, communicators, principled, open-minded, balanced, reflective and risk takers.

Yet another school may organise its schemes of work around Howard Gardner's 'five minds for the future', creating classroom learning opportunities to produce, over time:

- the disciplined mind, schooled in basic subjects such as history, science and art

- the synthesising mind, which can make sense of disparate pieces of information

- the creating mind, capable of asking new questions and finding imaginative answers

- the respectful mind, which shows an appreciation of different cultures

- the ethical mind, which enables one to behave responsibly as a worker and citizen.

One of the most interesting primary schools in the UK, Red Oaks Primary School in Swindon *(www.redoaks.org),* bases its memorable and exciting curriculum around what it terms as 'The Big Questions'. Staff and pupils together decide on a question, and ask themselves what they want to know in answer to that question. They then construct their curriculum accordingly, with detailed planning in relation to skills and knowledge acquisition and, vitally, progression from Nursery to Year 6.

The following are among the school's Big Questions, topics which have led to memorable series of lessons and excellent outcomes for pupils over many years:

- *Are there only seven wonders in the world?*
- *Does every picture tell a story?*
- *Have we left the past behind us?*
- *What will you do when I'm gone?*
- *What lies beneath and beyond?*
- *Do you have to be a hero to make a difference?*
- *What is great in Great Britain?*
- *Is there any justice in the world?*

This Swindon school has an on-site resource centre for children with special needs. It is no coincidence in my view that their curriculum is innovative. Thus, it is worth comment here that designated Special Schools in England, frequently not mentioned in the national debate on schooling, are in many ways at the cutting edge of curriculum development. Importantly, the best actively support the mainstream sector. The combination of a relative freedom from data-preoccupied outcomes and teachers working every day with children who manifest multiple learning difficulties, leads to experimentation, active classroom research and bespoke, personalised resources which are often of real cutting-edge quality.

In the end, it is for all primary schools to produce memorable experiences and rich opportunities for high quality learning, which have a decisive impact on children's well-being and self-esteem. Grasping the basics of language, mathematics and science is as vital as playing, learning to share and beginning to build that inner confidence as a lifelong learner.

Secondary curriculum

My mother left school aged 14 in the 1930s; I was at school in the 1960s with children who left aged 15. My teaching career began in south London in the early 1970s, coinciding with ROSLA – the raising of the school leaving age to 16. Students in secondary schools in the UK today will be in some kind of education and training until at least 18, finally bringing the country in line with its international competitors.

History suggests that with the passing of time, the extraordinary becomes the commonplace. The 14 year-old in 1936 deciding not to follow his father onto the land or into the mines but to pursue a career in the law was unusual. That 14 year-old today may well expect to be part of the country's near 50 per cent of 18 year-olds entering higher education, perhaps the first in his family to attend a university. That which once may have been unthinkable today passes almost as the norm.

Amongst education and business leaders in the UK there has been the ready acceptance (after initial knee-jerk opposition in some quarters – read the press files) that compulsory education and training to age 18 are desirable and necessary given the 21st century global workforce. Further, we do not even know the job titles of a quarter of all jobs which will exist in 2040.

Can secondary education (11-18) now stay the same? Does the curriculum need to change? For many secondary schools in England, particularly in areas where academic attainment has been chronically low, their focus has rightly been on improving basic literacy and mathematics skills through Years 7 and 8. Seeking to extend best primary practice has led to a modest degree of curriculum innovation.

Some schools have flirted with a modular curriculum, interesting programmes of electives and interventions, the timing of the school day to allow teenagers to start later, introduced world languages – but in truth, the average secondary school curriculum has changed little in my working life. The examination system calls the tune. As one secondary head remarked to me: 'We don't really have a curriculum vision. We do know what qualities and skills we want our students to have by the time they leave us. And all our clubs and visits are vital. But our curriculum is to all intents and purposes a series of exam syllabuses'. How right he is.

It is rare to visit a secondary school where students in the 14-18 age range are not spending the vast majority of their working days properly plugged into GCSE and A level courses. They are fulfilling the expectations of the universities, employers and parents. Inertia is potent, and change in this regard slow, even if it were desirable.

Worth commenting upon here is that the best independent schools in the UK and around the world follow similar curriculum and examination patterns; where they add particular value is often in the extracurricular richness. Abingdon School in Oxfordshire for example gives a clever message to its students by using the term 'The Other Half' to describe all activities that take place outside the classroom. Another independent school headmaster told me that his school's curriculum is a three-legged stool: first, the classroom; second, the 'playing fields'; third, and most importantly, those many and diverse clubs and activities which are generated by the students themselves and which build both confidence and social capital.

It will be interesting to see whether the establishment of more all-through (3-18) schools in England, under the free school and academy movement, leads to greater curriculum innovation and an active blurring of the long-standing primary/secondary divide. School 21 in the London borough of Newham is one worth watching *(www.school21.org.uk)*.

Academic-vocational apartheid

There remains one fundamental aspect of secondary provision which eludes us still in England, namely the proper provision of high quality vocational education and training. Maybe I am falling into a self-imposed trap by using the very term, but the academic-vocational apartheid which has bedevilled the English education system for generations needs addressing. Maybe the short answer is to leave any kind of so-called vocational *training* to the suitably equipped further education colleges, while secondary schools should satisfy themselves with a little vocational *education* – students learning *about* the world of work, not practising the skills required.

Historians often say that the one lesson of history is that we don't learn from history. Fifty years ago John Newsom and his colleagues presented to the government of the time a beautifully crafted, 300-page report titled 'Half Our Future', published 1963. Among its principal recommendations were these:

'The school programme in the final year ought to be deliberately outgoing – an invitation into the adult world of work and leisure.

The schools should resist external pressures to extend public examinations to pupils for who they are inappropriate.

Extended workshop and technical facilities should be provided whether wholly within schools or jointly with further education.'

Quaint language perhaps, but vocational education has long been a cause for concern in this country. It has often failed to command the confidence of employers, higher education and the general public. Indeed, ever since the 1944 Education Act, when the proposed technical schools were not developed on the scale originally envisaged, and then abandoned, it would be fair to judge that successive policy initiatives have never been more than partially effective. TVEI (Technical & Vocational Education Initiative) I remember well as a headteacher during the 1980s. The acronyms in this arena have come and gone with alarming speed. School-based diplomas in anything from engineering to health and beauty and retail have been the most recent very public failure.

In presenting his 1963 report John Newsom observed:

' *'Vocational' is a dangerous but indispensable word. It rightly means all that belongs to a man's calling. That itself is no doubt an old fashioned word, but at least it suggests that there is more to a job than money.'*

There must be many readers for whom, on a personal level, leaving school or college and pursuing a vocation meant taking up a calling: to teach, to nurse, to be an architect, to be a minister of the church. There may be other readers who readily and properly interpret 'vocational' as learning a skill or a trade.

The time has surely come for those of us charged with shaping the future for our young people to think of vocational education as preparing equally to be a careers adviser, a social worker, an electrician, a website designer, a hairdresser, a pilot. After all, what trades and professions (another telling linguistic divide) value alike is the ability to get things done to the highest standards.

Sadly, it remains the case that just 60 per cent of 16 year-olds secure at least five GCSE grade Cs, including English and mathematics. That statistic – 50 years on from Newsom's 'Half Our Future' – is not one the nation can be proud of. One cannot help wondering what we have been doing over the past five decades to provide a fulfilling secondary curriculum and fitting examination system. Things just have to get better, and quickly, when we benchmark the UK against many of the rising economies in the Pacific.

Secondary education – and its curriculum – needs a powerful twin-track approach over the coming decade.

One – schools must continue to take decisive steps to ensure that 90 plus per cent of all 16 year-olds attain at least a grade C in English and mathematics. This *can* be done by skilled teachers, building on raised standards in primary education, and with an unrelenting focus on raising expectations of our young people. This has to be matched by curriculum content which motivates and inspires.

Two – schools must bury the vocational/academic apartheid – and its accompanying vocabulary – which so bedevils our curriculum, and work relentlessly, with the wider community and business, to redefine what we mean by 'vocational'. Let us give the word a 21st century connotation which values equally the vocational – and *entrepreneurial* – skills of the pilot and the plumber, the car designer and the house builder, the chef and the teacher.

An historical end-piece

This chapter has ranged over past, present and future. As with all human endeavours, current generations walk upon the shoulders of those giants who preceded them.

One writer whose dangerous ideas have captured my heart is A. C. Benson. The next chapter opens with his absorbing words, and I close this chapter with a few lines from his immaculate pen. Here writing in 1902 overlooking the playing fields of Eton, he reflects on the educated man and does it matter what we teach. Crafted in a grammar of the era, I commend *The Schoolmaster* to all who share my fascination with classrooms and schools of any period.

The nation appears to me to be mainly preoccupied with two ambitions: success, which in many cases is identical to wealth; and manly conduct, which is a combination of aptitude for outdoor exercises with the practice of wholesome virtues. To put it in academical terms, the national ideal seems to be a mixture of the Hebraistic and the Spartan systems – national prosperity, with a certain standard of right conduct, and physical prowess. It seems that the Athenian ideal – that of strong intellectual capacity – is left out of sight altogether.

My idea of an intellectual person is one whose mind is alive to ideas; who is interested in politics, religion, science, history, literature; who knows enough to wish to know more, and to listen if he cannot talk; a person who is not at the mercy of a new book, a leading article, or the chatter of an irresponsible outsider; a person who is not insular, provincial, narrow-minded, contemptuous.

Arthur Christopher Benson

Chapter 7

The cocktail of great classrooms

A school lesson should be of the nature of a dramatic performance, from which some interest and amusement may be expected; while at the same time there must be solid and business-like work done. Variety of every kind should be attempted; the blackboard should be used, there should be some simple jesting, there should be some anecdote, some disquisition, and some allusion if possible to current events, and the result should be that the boys should not only feel that they have put away some definite knowledge under lock and key, but also that they have been in contact with a lively and more mature mind. Exactly in what proportion the cauldron should be mingled, and what its precise ingredients should be, must be left to the taste and tact of the teacher.

The Schoolmaster, A.C. Benson

What more is there to be observed about teaching than this masterful description from Eton College in the early years of the 20th century? A statement about the infinite variety of teaching at its best, no one-size-fits-all formula. When all is said and written about schools, it's the classrooms which matter most. This is where students and teachers together spend a good part of their waking hours.

I have enjoyed a 40-year love affair with classrooms. I find them fascinating.

What is it that makes them so intriguing, so diverse, so endlessly unpredictable? Why are they just the greatest of venues, full of laughter and stories that no other workplace matches? What *does* create the cocktail of the high performing classroom? I use the term 'classroom' in a generic sense: it includes workshops, laboratories, gymnasia, sports fields, outdoor settings, dance studios, music practice rooms – wherever that great double act which is teaching and learning is taking place.

As an observer, coach, inspector or reviewer my simple definition of an excellent lesson is a lesson I just don't want to leave. I want to know where the teacher and pupils are going next and what their individual 'learning moments' will lead to.

English and literacy

The current inspection framework in the UK places a strong emphasis on key skills in schools. The definition of outstanding teaching makes explicit that the teaching of reading, writing, communication and mathematics must be 'highly effective and cohesively planned and implemented.' And this must surely be a core expectation in any classroom in the world.

The same emphasis features in the 2012 Teachers' Standards. All teachers are expected to have a clear understanding of appropriate teaching strategies for early reading and mathematics. Equally, teachers of whatever age range or subject are expected to promote 'high standards of literacy, articulacy and the correct use of standard English'.

Thirdly, the 2014 National Curriculum in England places great weight on the place of high quality English teaching, including the following key points:

'The national curriculum for English aims to ensure that all pupils:

- *read easily, fluently and with good understanding*
- *acquire a wide vocabulary, an understanding of grammar and knowledge of linguistic conventions for reading, writing, and spoken language*
- *write clearly, accurately and coherently*
- *are competent in the arts of speaking and listening.'*

These expectations from Ofsted, the Teachers' Standards and the 2014 National Curriculum are rightly highlighting *the* foundation stone in any classroom. Without a child being able to access the printed word, progress across the curriculum will be negligible. Teachers must give young people the dignity of being able to speak, read and write with fluency to make their way in the fascinating global society they will be shaping.

Checklist One

In the most effective and engaging English lessons I regularly see some of the following in action:

1. Pupils being *expected* to answer questions in developed phrases rather than just monosyllables, from nursery onwards.

2. Teachers giving more time for pupils to develop fuller oral responses to questions posed.

3. Teachers enabling pupils to pose questions of one another, in order that pupils practise their sounds and speech patterns.

4. Direct and regular intervention/correction from staff in how children speak and pronounce their letters.

5. Volunteer staff and governors giving time to small groups of children in order to develop their conversation, vocabulary and basic social skills.

6. The development of structured and regular drama/acting opportunities in which children are expected to project their voice and practise speaking at length, with good eye contact.

7. The regular use of limericks/couplets/verses/short poems being set to be learned by heart and for recitation in class groups; parents can be involved creatively in this.

8. The consistent use of established EAL techniques (pattern, repetition, consolidation, elaboration) with children, particularly boys, whose first language is English.

9. The regular use of short dictations, across the curriculum, and with an emphasis on keen listening and high quality presentation of writing.

10. A focus on how children are actually holding a pencil/pen and how they are forming their letters on a consistent basis.

Inspiring and vibrant teaching

In great classrooms in any school there is always that judicious balance of the fun and fundamentals of learning. Enjoyment, humour and warm relationships abound. So too does an unequivocal focus on practising basic and higher order skills. Aspirational teachers accept no substitute.

Excellent teachers create climates for learning which engender confidence and motivation among the learners. Critically, there is no fear of failure because teachers and pupils alike support one another's triumphs and disasters. Opportunities for risk taking, exploration of new knowledge and concepts, and experimentation permeate. Learners' potential is spotted and encouraged. In the true sense of the word, education – 'to lead out' – underpins the learning environment.

Ask any group of students, from age 7 to 17, what makes for effective classroom learning and they talk about the teacher who loves their subject and shares that passion with their pupils through rich tasks and activities. To use a word that has sadly gone out of fashion in some quarters, it is the promotion of *scholarship* that matters.

Pupils are infected by the enthusiasms of their teachers. Pupils deeply respect the teacher who has a breadth and depth of knowledge that they themselves can, at their age, only dream of and aspire to. Just think for a moment of the teachers you remember with affection from your own school days. Yes, it will be the teacher who knew and valued you as a person. It will also be a mathematician, a biologist, a linguist or a musician whose own scholarship was not in doubt, who shared their ambitions and enthusiasms.

Memorable classrooms are vibrant places where what is on the walls, windows, floor and ceiling matters. The teachers have given thought to learning prompts, keywords, photos (taken by pupils) celebrating achievement, and displays of high quality pupils' work to which their peers can aspire.

Furthermore, book and technological resources are accessible and fit for purpose. The portable IT device is present, no more nor less important than a pair of scissors. It is a tool for learning which each generation of young people masters more skilfully than the majority of its teachers.

I once asked a group of talented 13 year-olds to draw images of what made for effective and less effective lessons. Intriguingly, they set to on their sugar paper to draw a series of boxes with expanding and contracting heads. The more effective a lesson became, they charted with their colour pens, the larger the pupils' heads and the smaller the teacher's head. They were seeking to point out that the teacher begins the lines of enquiry, giving space for learners to continue the journey.

Checklist Two

What I look for in a great classroom: scholarship, love of learning and intellectual curiosity. In these classrooms children:

- make sense of and deal creatively and positively with the circumstances of their lives, their current environment and the world at large

- command language in its major forms and use them readily, competently and easily to serve their purposes

- observe critically; assemble evidence; analyse and reflect on what they have discovered; draw conclusions based on evidence and thoughts; test their conclusions as far as possible; adapt and restructure these according to the outcomes of testing; communicate their conclusions to others; hold them up to scrutiny and review in the light of discussion and informed commentary

- learn to think, respond and behave according to the form and conventions of major disciplines; that is, they are able, where necessary, to act as scientists, historians, geographers, technologists and mathematicians would

- solve problems: they can engage with and bring reason and practical resource to bear on the challenges and problems of human existence

- possess a critical faculty which enables them to distinguish between the substantial and the trivial, the genuine and the spurious, and to identify the crucial points in argument, data, literature and presentation.

Skilful orchestration

A hallmark of fine classrooms is that time within lessons is skilfully orchestrated. Teachers do not rattle on at pace, galloping through the scheme of work for fear of running out of time. Rather, they deliver narratives and explanations at a speed consistent with pupils' understanding and internalising new concepts, knowledge and skills. Young minds are afforded time to reflect, ponder and be challenged as they tackle a demanding activity – and that of course leads to manifest quick progress by pupils.

Teaching and learning are a mutually dependent double act. The effective teacher helps pupils, through various techniques, to think about the progress they are making: daily, weekly, and over a term or a year.

The teacher and pupil reflecting on progress together, through marking and dialogue, identify next steps in learning and what particular support or extension might be required to ensure the pupil's individual needs are met. This is as true of an infant teacher observing the development of fine motor skills, as it is of the GCSE history teacher concentrating on improving essay writing skills.

In the same way that a hand surgeon needs to have detailed knowledge of the nerves, tendons and arteries of that part of the body, so the professional teacher needs excellent technical know-how. The primary specialist has a clear understanding of cognitive development in seven year-olds, and how different approaches to number bonds need to be adopted to secure positive progress in mathematics in a Year 2 classroom. Equally, the A level teacher of chemistry brings to their seminar group a secure command of organic reaction pathways, so that students can approach a demanding concept from different directions in order to grasp its complexities.

And skilful orchestration of time is all about skilful differentiation. All teachers know that just about the hardest aspect of teaching a class is getting 'the learning moments' right for individuals' different abilities and aptitudes – what is commonly described as matching learning activities to the needs of pupils.

Checklist Three

What I see teachers doing skilfully in well-differentiated lessons:

1. Knowing pupils' prior attainment and knowledge of a subject
2. Meticulous tracking of pupils' progress in different skills
3. Thinking through which pupils work best with others, and the optimum size for effective group work
4. Judging when independent learning will best deepen knowledge and understanding
5. Knowing when best to harness the library, film, internet to expand pupils' thinking
6. Setting up one-to-one catch-up and intervention sessions, before, during and after school
7. Setting meaningful homework, well-scaffolded for individual needs
8. Knowing what factors inhibit progress and seeking to remove those barriers promptly
9. Identifying special needs such as poor hand-eye co-ordination, delayed cognitive development, temporary medical problems
10. Practising 'differentiation down' to ensure higher attainers are extended in their learning.

Talk less, do less

I fondly say that all teachers need a chaise longue in their classrooms, so that just occasionally they can sit back and admire what they have created – and thereby enable the pupils to work harder than the teacher!

Best practice for promoting excellent progress is certainly rooted in the teacher who expects, from time to time, to talk and do less than her pupils. Take for example the Grade 6 teacher I observed who, in introducing a week's lessons on Darwin and natural selection, shared her lesson plans with the class and explained how each day one pair of pupils was going to run the lesson starter, another would lead the mini-plenary, how another pair would conclude the session and set appropriate homework.

To teach is to learn: the best teachers enable their pupils to make significant progress and practise their own articulacy on a regular, well planned basis. Consistent with the age and growing maturity of the pupil, creative teachers encourage independence. This independence is demonstrated by pupils taking a responsible and conscientious approach to their classwork and homework. It will not happen by magic. Effective teachers nudge, cajole and model independent learning habits. In common with good parents, they give 'roots and wings' to children.

In *The Learning Game*, one of the most readable and thoughtfully observed books written on the craft of the classroom, Jonathan Smith sums up trenchantly the balance between pupil and teacher dominated classroom commerce:

In a lesson - as in a good conversation, as indeed in life - you need to be light on your feet, to know when to change gear, when to change the angles and when to change the tone. It helps to have a back-up plan, a lighter or different fall-back idea. You have to be able to alter your response; to know when to stop eye-contact, when to let someone else take centre stage, when to disengage or to suggest that enough is enough on a particular topic. You need to know when to talk and when to listen. Many teachers talk too much and listen too little. Some teachers listen to too much waffle and don't cut in enough. The trick is to know which is which.

The best lessons

In the Chief Inspector's 2013 report on schools and classrooms in England*, the following are identified as common misconceptions, leading to less effective teaching:

Pace – A belief that the faster the lesson, the better the learning. While pace is important – pupils may lose concentration in a slow lesson – teachers concentrate too often on the pace of the activity rather than the amount of learning.

The number of activities – Some teachers believe that the more activities they can cram into the lesson, the more effective it will be. This is often counterproductive, as activities are changed so often that pupils do not complete tasks and learning is not consolidated or extended.

Over-detailed and bureaucratic lesson plans – Excessive detail within these plans can cause teachers to lose sight of the central focus on pupils' learning.

An inflexible approach to planning lessons – Some school policies insist that all lesson plans should always follow the same structure, no matter what is being taught. The key consideration should be the development of pupils' learning rather than sticking rigidly to a format.

Constant review of learning in lessons – In lessons observed, significant periods of time were spent by teachers on getting pupils to articulate their learning before they had completed enough work. Indeed, inspectors observed lessons where pupils were asked to self- or peer-assess work before they had been able to complete more than a sentence or two.

*(HMCI, Ofsted 2012/13)

These five points are well worth reflecting on when seeking to achieve best practice. We all learn what *not* to do as key starting points for what *to do* well.

The same HMCI report includes three useful case studies of outstanding practice, which share the common classroom characteristics of high expectations, detailed subject knowledge, good and attentive behaviour, and an unremitting focus on what children are expected to learn.

Case Study 1

From the outset of a Year 3 literacy lesson, the teacher established a very 'business-like' atmosphere. Pupils had resources at the ready, were highly attentive and worked briskly. The teacher had high expectations of all pupils; they were all to review and apply what they knew about the use of modal verbs. Pupils listened intently as the teacher recapped previous learning, using a story to prompt the class to identify examples and justify them. There were excellent opportunities for speaking and listening, as pupils identified the correct spoken language for each example. The teacher challenged all pupils, including the most able, by asking individuals to reflect on her detailed marking of the work in their books. Pupils appreciated this and rose to the challenge of answering the precise questions that the teacher had posed. Next steps in learning were clarified for all; each pupil pursued their own target, made rapid progress and reached above average attainment levels. In preparing the lesson, teaching and marking, this teacher drew on excellent subject knowledge to make sure that all pupils understood about modal verbs, and could use them in speech and in writing.
(Ofsted 2013)

Case Study 2

In a Year 6 science lesson, the teacher had evidently high expectations of all pupils. The teacher led the pupils through the detailed workings of the human digestive system, with short, sharp direct inputs and a series of challenges set for the pupils. During the lesson, pupils were asked to explore different models of the digestive system, while the teacher and teaching assistants reinforced pupils' learning and extended it by asking pupils to predict what would happen next and encouraging them to question. Pupils were expected to be curious and became engrossed, applying the correct technical language such as pancreas, oesophagus and bile. They learned rapidly, showing their thirst for knowledge and answered questions such as 'Does food just slide down the oesophagus? What other factors may be assisting?' This lesson used skilled teaching to enthuse pupils while teaching them key scientific knowledge. (Ofsted 2013)

Case Study 3

Year 11 English students were studying J.B. Priestley's An Inspector Calls. Students listened attentively and quietly as the teacher opened the lesson by explaining key features of evaluative writing. Her talk included an excellent example of an evaluative sentence, and students were challenged to come up with examples of their own. Following this, students were set to work on exploring the text, and during their evaluative writing the teacher cross-examined individuals, using searching questions to provoke a deeper level of knowledge and understanding. The work set had been meticulously planned and each student was mindful of their target grades and knew what was expected of them. Although this was a tightly planned lesson, the teacher responded flexibly to students' questions, allowing the lesson's 'direction of travel' to shift so that she could fill gaps in the students' knowledge and understanding. (Ofsted 2013)

These descriptions capture concisely many of the hallmarks of outstanding teaching and learning. For my own part when I think about the best teachers, I think of the epitaph of the great 17th century architect Sir Christopher Wren: 'If you seek his monument, look around you'.

Confident teachers in vibrant classrooms, tellingly, teach with their doors open. They can beckon any passing observer to see the cocktail of pupils' progress and enjoyment in learning right across their classrooms: from detailed record-keeping and regular, incisive marking to the quality of their wall displays, oral interventions and digressions, and the expertise and passion they bring to a subject.

In particular, making up the cocktail of memorable classrooms:

- great lessons are all about richness of task and searching questions, rooted in teachers' excellent subject knowledge and passion to share that wisdom with children and young people

- there is no single formula for success, teachers create their own – remember A.C.Benson's 'taste and tact'
- pupils' prior knowledge of a subject is endlessly surprising, and skilled teachers harness it powerfully
- opportunities for extending and deepening learning are 'taken' not 'missed', by teachers and students
- timely digression and intervention promote memorable learning moments
- high quality marking from teachers fuels students' rapid progress
- doing more of the same does not transform standards of achievement and lesson outcomes– doing *differently* can
- the best teachers are children at heart
- observing the best lessons, you just don't want them to end!

Checklist Four

Questions to ask when co-observing a Year 6 primary classroom, thinking about the cocktail of excellent practice.

1. What are your first impressions of the learning environment?
   - is it light, airy and the right temperature for learning?
   - does the classroom, and the areas around it, reflect the range of Y6/upper primary work? What is special, or striking, about this work?
   - is the classroom arranged so that children can be involved in discussions and also use their workspace to write, design and implement?
   - how do the children react to your presence as a visitor? Are they happy to talk and explain?

2. In what ways does the style of teaching and learning reflect that this is a Year 6 class and therefore distinctive in terms of the completion of the primary stage of learning?

3. How is furniture configured? Where does the teacher position her/himself?

4. To what extent do the children take control of their learning and how able are they to explore a range of learning areas? Are the children aware of what will come next in terms of their move to the secondary stage?

5. In the time you are in the room, count the minutes (a) the teacher talks (b) children converse with a proper focus. Is the teacher working harder than the students? Are the children responding easily and readily to the task/stimuli provided?

6. What evidence can you see of Year 6's independent learning skills? If the teacher left the room, would the children continue to work on the current task?

7. Is the level of work appropriate for the more able learners and is it sufficiently demanding? Has the work been effectively scaffolded, whilst retaining an intrinsic interest/challenge for those who have learning or personal management difficulties?

8. Is homework or other independent study/research important to the lesson? Has there been some form of lead-in and are there possibilities for extension?

9. What evidence is there of (a) fun (b) scholarship (c) intriguing digressions (d) teacher sharing personal enthusiasms?

10. How well does the teacher demonstrate his/her own specialist subject knowledge? Does s/he extend horizons and leave students magically wondering?

Checklist Five

Questions to ask when observing a Year 11 secondary classroom, thinking about the cocktail of excellent practice.

1. What are your first impressions of the learning environment?
    - is it light, airy and the right temperature for learning?
    - does the room celebrate the specialist subject being taught?
    - does the room celebrate Year 11 work?
    - how do the students react to your presence as a visitor?

2. In what ways does the style of teaching and learning reflect that this is a Year 11 class and not a Year 7 class? (eg How is furniture configured? Where does the teacher position her/himself?)

3. In the time you are in the room, count the minutes (a) the teacher talks (b) students converse with a proper focus? Is the teacher working harder than the students?

4. What evidence can you see of Year 11's independent learning skills? If the teacher left the room, would students' focus continue?

5. Are the students teaching?

6. Is the level of work appropriate for more able students, irrespective of mixed-ability or setted group? If not, how would you make it more demanding?

7. How has homework led into this lesson? How is homework/further independent study/research following up the lesson?

8. What evidence is there of (a) fun (b) scholarship (c) intriguing digressions (d) teacher sharing personal enthusiasms?

9. How well does the teacher demonstrate his/her own specialist subject knowledge? Does s/he extend horizons and leave students magically wondering?

10. How creatively are book/technology resources harnessed to stimulate students' interest and extend their skills and knowledge?

11. Can you tell from looking at books/folders whether students fully understand syllabus demands ('the story of their learning')? Is there a difference in the quality of note-taking and storage, say between girls and boys?

12. Targets for individuals and groups – are they in place? Is marking formative and advising how a student can improve from say, grade B to grade A? Do students know what A* quality in the subject looks like?

Chapter 8

Blinks

The ability to focus attention on important things is a defining characteristic of intelligence.

Robert J. Shiller

Keeping the school under review

Working at Pimlico School in central London in the 1980s, I first became aware of the power of the media and at that time of the *Evening Standard* newspaper. This was an era, almost forgotten now, of public buildings including schools being regular targets for bomb hoaxes. The Irish Republican Army were in full cry. How personally difficult and professionally brave a decision it must have been for headteachers not to evacuate their schools, almost on a daily basis, as hoax phone calls were received.

These were halcyon days when schools were 'open' – you could as a parent or a member of the public just walk in. One day in my role as Head of Year I walked into the boys' toilets to chase out a miscreant, to be confronted by a newspaper photographer taking photos of wall graffiti, all part of a story to discredit the school. It seems incredible now, but given the school's closeness to Westminster and given many journalists' notorious laziness to move beyond the SW1 bubble, our glass-house building was a natural magnet for media interest. In truth, a too London-centric lazy press remains today.

As a middle leader I was part of a working group looking at how we could best promote the many excellent strengths of the school to parents and the local community, partly countering negative and unwarranted publicity; Pimlico offered, for example, pioneering provision for gifted musicians across London, a sort of free Yehudi Menuhin School. The Inner London Education Authority (ILEA) had recently published a booklet titled 'Keeping the school under review', innovative in the late 1970s when the notion of an annual self-evaluation document for a school was altogether new.

It struck me then as a middle leader that writing for the headteacher my own short report on the achievements of the 315 pupils in my year group would be a good thing, by way of self-appraisal if nothing else. I have the annual reports still. It was all very ad hoc, a system of school self-review in its infancy.

Now the self-evaluation business has come a long way since then, more sophisticated, polished and data-rich, although has at times risked turning into a mini-industry for consultants. Ask any successful headteacher around the world and she or he will express the virtues of the process and outcome of regular self-evaluation across a school, usually with the caveat about carefully managed paper-work. One might say with confidence that it has become an integral tool of successful school leadership.

What I learned subsequently as a deputy head in London and then as a headteacher in Oxfordshire is that self-evaluation is fine as far as it goes. In the hands of wise professionals, if the process of gathering such documents together is well run, the finished product presents a series of shapshots which serve to celebrate current practices and trigger further improvements.

It is true of course that inspection systems developed over the past twenty years have seen self-evaluation forms in one shape or another as an important starting point for external inspection. Indeed, they have assumed a bold acronym: SEF. But put aside inspection for a moment. How can a school most effectively validate its own judgements on a regular basis? My answer lies in *Blinks*.

Blinks

In 2005, Ofsted decided that a Proportionate Inspection Pilot (PIP) should be launched, in which I had the privilege to play a lead role with regard to inspecting mainly good and outstanding schools for just a day. The inspectorate tested the model robustly and then moved wisely (in the best interests of headteachers and inspectors) to the two-day model of inspection which schools experience currently. The model ebbs and flows.

The following is taken from my June 2005 diary, the names and locations of the schools have been changed:

A tale of two countries

A hot midsummer day. Quiet, still. The village of Magby, with 50 houses, deep in rural Essex. A maypole next to the school site. An 1860s school-house, imaginatively converted to provide for 56 children. Years 3 – 6 are taught in the main room; infants and Reception in the smaller classroom. What was formerly the home of the schoolteacher upstairs has become staffroom, secretary's office, music room and store. A good school, with one or two outstanding features – we are all agreed. Given the no-notice of the inspection, the afternoon was the summer fete, something my colleague inspector had never seen in ten years of Ofsted work – 'because schools rearrange them if inspectors are coming'. And at the school fete, run by the children of course, every dimension of Every Child Matters was writ large. So proud of their school, such promise in these young people. Parents were present to tell us their views of the school. The oldest man in the village described to me his own years in the schoolroom (no laptops) between 1926 and 1933, before leaving to work on the land – and how the children now invite him regularly for coffee and tales of former times. Memorable.

***

Maryland Primary in the heart of Sheffield, set at an intersection of roads which generates a relentless buzz of screeched tyres. The school has featured in national newspapers in former days, 'for the wrong reasons' I'm reliably informed. An equally hot day in June. 680 primary children with a dozen languages between them and families across continents, exuberant, full of joy, and unfailingly courteous to a four-strong team of inspectors. A Victorian, two-decker building, a riot of colour and display celebrating rich cultural diversity. We agree – a satisfactory school, with some good features; standards on entry well below national averages. The headteacher, not phased by the no-notice inspection, hosts a community health day: at 9.30am sixty families are in the main hall enjoying aromatherapy sessions, courses on diet and how to take blood pressure readings. One seasoned inspector remarks that Ofsted have never seen such events, 'because it would have disturbed the inspection'. The ECM agenda in practice. Breaktimes and lunchtimes in the cramped tarmac playground are a reminder that urban Britain in the 21st century, as seen through the eyes of children, is a wonderfully harmonious place to be. And it will be just like this again tomorrow. Memorable.

***

I maintain that very good inspectors working with very good headteachers can conduct a fair and full inspection of a school of pretty well any size within a day. Focused on the key aspects of pupils' achievement and well-being, the classroom and what leadership is doing - no more than a couple of inspectors can do the job, and make very effective use of public money.

At the same time as this inspection experience I came across Malcolm Gladwell's book *Blink,* in which he explores the power of judgments being made in the blink of an eye – and can we trust those important judgements? Though not a book at all about schools and teaching, he does describe memorably how a person watching a silent ten-second videoclip of a teacher he or she has never met will reach conclusions about how good a teacher is, that are very similar to those of a student who has sat in the teacher's class for an entire semester.

So in establishing the National Education Trust in 2006 I was determined to bring the notion of Blink to primary, special and secondary schools across the country and in my international work, ambitious for Blink to become a vital part of schools' self-reviewing processes. Eight years on, and thus it has proved.

Blink offers a model of review, whether in an early years' setting, children's centre, school or college. Blink is essentially:

ONE   A fresh pairs of eyes on a familiar location; the Blink is tailored and bespoke to a particular context

TWO   Asking questions – and further searching questions – about established practice in order that (a) effective practice is championed and (b) less effective practice is challenged, with suggestions given for improvement and development

THREE A style of working that makes people in the given workplace feel better about what they are doing as a result of meeting and talking through their work with the person leading the Blink.

How the Blink is conducted is as important as *what* is reviewed.

Further, Blink has the following key features of a robust industrial model, applicable in any number of sectors or settings.

- it is conducted by *high quality* practitioners

- it is *sustainable* through a training programme which enables fellow practitioners to be properly inducted and thus able to conduct Blinks

- it is able to be *scaled up* in different contexts, national and international, through systematic quality assurance

- it can be *adapted* to different cultural contexts and for different purposes, with the core purpose of reviewing, making judgements, championing good practice, and indicating further improvements: supporting self-evaluation.

(For further information about Blink, and training for teachers and school leaders, contact *director@nationaleducationtrust.net*)

Blinks in action: a day in the life

8.00   Reviewer(s) meets senior team to set a context and to run through any documentation that has been sent prior to the day. The focus for the day is affirmed – eg. independent learning, oracy and literacy, mathematics

9.00   Lesson observations across the school, perhaps 15 minutes in each classroom, and some co-observations with staff

12.00   Walk with senior leader to look at, for example, outdoor learning

12.30   Meet with small group of students to explore their views on the day's focused topic

Reviewer has lunch and gathers thoughts.

2.00   Meetings with middle leaders, groups of teachers, governors, to discuss the day's focused topic

3.30   Reviewer meets with head to rehearse feedback to staff: what are the important messages for staff to hear which celebrate what is good and prompt discussion for improvements?

4.00   Feedback and discussion with staff; feedback to the reviewer on how the process has been for staff.

A written report, no more than an agreed two sides of A4, is sent to the school within five days. And that's it, until the next visit, commissioned by the school to build on what the first Blink has identified.

A Blink report on a primary school
Turche Hill Primary
Blink: 12 January 2014

Focus: establishing one school, following the merger of infant and junior in September 2013

Part A

The following features characterised effective teaching and learning:

- Warm relationships between staff and children, with children feeling valued and enjoying their time in school
- Well planned and organised classrooms and lessons, with imaginative deployment of resources; children handled resources with care and respect

- Engaging activities which led to a strong focus from pupils
- Effective use of portable devices to broaden styles of learning
- A wide range of curriculum opportunities evident in tasks, in exercise books, and in classroom and corridor displays
- Positive focus and clear sense of purpose when children were working individually, in groups or as a whole class
- Good teacher knowledge, enthusiastically presented, which led to probing questioning and children being asked to think outside their comfort zones
- VCOP imaginatively displayed, and harnessed for pupils in lessons
- Time well managed so that pupils were given enough time to complete practical, fun activities to a high quality
- Thoughtful and skilled inclusion of children with special needs
- Good photographic records of children's progress in the early years
- An excellent feature of the school is the way staff have approached marking in pupils' books. There is consistency in the way formative and summative comments are presented, and there is 'next best step' marking of high quality across the core subjects. In some classes this is being extended by children writing notes in exercise books to indicate how well they are understanding a new idea or skill.

The staff are to be congratulated on this aspect of their practice; it serves children well if they know there is this kind of consistent approach right through the primary school.

Part B

The staff might wish to consider the following, as you shape the single primary school:

- *What should every flourishing classroom at TH Primary have?* Mindful that some classrooms are more readily shaped for display, nonetheless look at the best practice around the school and share it.
- How might book corners promote love of books more effectively, perhaps with cushions, drapes and book reviews by children?
- How might VCOP displays be developed in every classroom? (A new dictionary stock is required, particularly so that junior children have access to high quality ones.)
- Could every classroom have some high quality children's written work on display, to which others can aspire? This work should be changed each month, and then perhaps go on display in the halls.

- In classroom activities, what is the optimum size of group for children to work in, to achieve consistently very good learning?

- How might photographs of work in action – taken by children – be a regular feature of classroom and corridor display? (There is often in schools best practice to be learned from early years' profiles.)

- What steps might be taken to raise expectations of written work in exercise books, so that children present their best work consistently? (Given the quality of marking in the school, this should not be difficult to achieve.)

- Thinking about community outreach – local, national, international – what more could be done to feature global issues and children's awareness of other cultures? How are globes and maps of the world used across the school?

- How might staff maximise opportunities for children to practise their oral language skills? Expect them to respond in phrases and sentences rather than teachers accepting just one word answers.

- How might there be sharper differentiation in all lessons, particularly for the most able pupils? What does a potential Level 5 writer need to experience from Year 3 onwards?

Part C

Turche Hill Primary is perhaps best described today as 'a sleeping giant'. The new school is one of the largest primaries in Leicester, with good indoor and outdoor facilities and the promise of some further investment. I would urge the school to capitalise on its very size. With the large staff reflecting on their considerable talents, what might the school specialise in and carve out a distinctive reputation around? For example, there is certainly scope to look at the potential of mixed-age learning. Other curriculum areas, led by teaching and support staff, might become specialisms, and a decision here may help shape any future building work.

There is a sense of a strong school community, with children arriving each day wanting to learn. There is significant potential ahead.

My thanks to children and staff for their warm welcome and openness to discussion about the future of the school.

Roy Blatchford. (Names and places have been changed)

***

A note on lesson observations

Studying an E. coli bacterium under a microscope in a laboratory does not fundamentally change that bacterium. Observe a sub-atomic particle then the observation itself changes that particle's properties. Do lesson observations by a live observer (headteacher, colleague, inspector, coach) suffer a similar fate?

As someone who has observed many thousands of lessons in classrooms across the world, I often find myself debating that question with teachers, school leaders, administrators and inspectors. There are those who would argue that the very presence of an observer changes the nature of the dynamic between the teacher and the taught. Maybe or maybe not. From sitting, kneeling and standing in all corners of laboratories, studios and playing fields, I would say as a general rule that if the observer is experienced then they will capture the everyday commerce of the classroom, more or less intact. There will always be exceptions - and they are often quietly amusing, frequently causing a quick wry smile to pass between teacher and observer.

Much hinges on the culture of a school. The best schools 'teach with the door open', either literally or metaphorically. What the teachers in those schools are saying is: 'Come in and see what I'm doing. I'm proud of it'. Walk as a visitor into classrooms in such an open culture and, whether accompanied by the headteacher, the chair of governors or the bursar, the students don't blink. Move along a mathematics corridor in a secondary school where teachers teach with doors closed, and yes of course when you knock and enter, there is temporary change. And some schools choose it that way, they like visitors to be formally welcomed - that is their proper decision.

In many, many classrooms I enter when conducting Blinks, such is the richness of the task which the teacher has set, and such is the resulting focus by the pupils, that truly the observed have not even noticed the observer. Confident teachers are certainly not thrown by another consenting adult in the room. A newly qualified teacher observed recently to me: 'Every time I am observed, I get better'.

One caveat: it would be right to acknowledge that in the course of a formal school inspection, students and staff alike are more relaxed on day two than they are in the first few hours of day one. In one experience of leading an inspection, with a large team of inspectors, of a school of 10,000 students over a week, the sheer scale of the place meant that we were never any more than passing butterflies. Rightly so. We captured that school's story with especial pleasure.

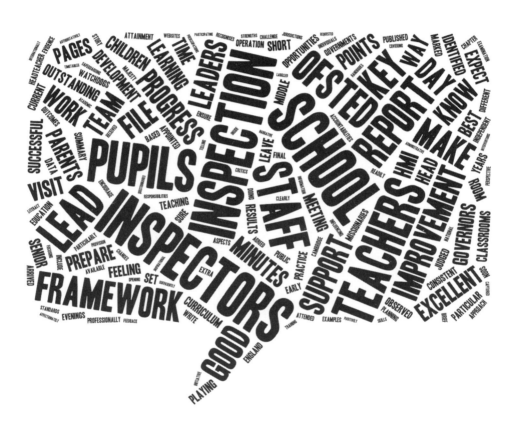

Chapter 9
Leading inspections

Circular To Staff

There is to be a General Inspection by Her Majesty's Inspectors. May I urge that all books be marked up to date, that examples of the children's best work are readily available, most of it pinned to the walls, that the children be warned about their deportment in and out of the classroom and that nobody is allowed 'to leave the room' during those three days. The bell must be rung a minute or two later for playtime going-out and two or three minutes earlier for coming-in. Have a ready supply of pencils sharpened so that nobody is left without one. On no account argue with the Inspectors but agree enthusiastically and without demur, declaring that any suggestions they make are excellent and will be put into operation immediately.

The Harpole Report J.L. Carr

Watchdogs and missionaries: a short history

In 1893 the diary of one of Her Majesty's Inspectors (HMI) in England records a visit to a rural school. The inspector had set out early on horse from his office in Cambridge. He arrived at the school to find, as his note of visit records, 'the children playing harmoniously together in the playground'. He got off his horse and looked through the window of the one-room school to see the teacher asleep next to the warm stove in the middle of the room. The children were playing so well together that he did not wake the teacher before going on his way. He simply recorded in his diary: 'Arrived at 11.15 am, left at 11.35 am.'

Now the inspection of schools has come a long way since then.

It was originally in 1839 that the first two HMI in England were appointed. They were seen as *watchdogs* (particularly on how money on schools was being spent) and *missionaries*, and were expected to be the eyes and ears of the Department for Education based in London. To a large extent the nature of the early inspectorate was governed by the attitude of the church, and inspectors were only appointed where archbishops and bishops agreed. Of the 93 inspectors appointed up to 1870, at least 80 had attended Oxford or Cambridge universities, and almost 70 per cent were clergymen.

In the 19th century of course, teachers were paid according to the test results of their pupils; the inspectors played a large part in the so-called 'payment by results' system and thus soon came to be feared. Further, Rules for Teachers were inspected:

Teachers each day will fill lamps, trim the wicks and clean chimneys.

Each morning teachers will bring a bucket of water and a scuttle of coal for the day's session.

Men teachers may take one evening each week for courting purposes, or two evenings a week if they attend church regularly.

Women teachers who marry or engage in unseemly conduct will be dismissed.

Every teacher should lay aside a goodly sum of his earnings for his benefit during his declining years so that he will not become a burden on society.

Rules For Teachers 1872

Throughout the 20th century the influence of HMI grew significantly, with inspectors not only visiting schools, but designing classrooms and buildings, writing curriculum advice, and clearly influencing what should be taught and how it should be taught. They were often affectionately viewed as diplomats and detectives.

With the election in 1979 of Prime Minister Margaret Thatcher came a fundamental challenge to the long-held traditions of the public services. While her governments sought to make changes in how the nation's schools behaved and performed, it was not until 1992 that Ofsted was created, absorbing the role of HMI. Gone was their missionary role of spreading best practice; arriving was an emphasis on inspectors as watchdogs.

Amongst all the inspections on individual schools carried out during the twentieth century up to this point, few were ever published so that parents and the wider public could read them. Indeed, visits to school were sporadic and lacked real system as we would recognise it today; in 30 years between 1960 and 1990, as a headteacher in four different schools, my father met just four HMI, each for no more than a day. He can still remember what they remarked on. All that changed in 1992. Suddenly every school which was inspected received a 60-page Ofsted report written about its every movement, and published to the local community. This coincided with the first publication of examination league tables. Competition between schools became the name of the game. Parents then came to look at websites and compare schools.

What the inspectorate soon learned during the 1990s was that wordy and descriptive reports had little real impact on parents and indeed teachers. Within a few years, short, punchy 'less is more' reports, strong on evaluation, came into being, and current Ofsted reports are yet another iteration in this vein.

Now Ofsted may have its critics in England but its inspection frameworks have been taken up and modified in many countries around the world. In my direct experience many governments have taken the 'improvement through inspection' strapline and shaped it for their own ends. In contrast, a number have decided that regular, formal inspection, with published reports, is not the way to lift educational standards. Internationally, we are where we are, rooted in different cultural norms.

Finally, by way of perspective, the Independent Schools Inspection (ISI) framework is worth a reference. As one who has inspected using this framework it has many merits, albeit operating in a relatively small sector. Most attractive is the fact that the framework inspects schools against their *aims* first, their outcomes second – a wholly sane approach in my view and, more importantly, in the view of experienced headteachers.

To get a flavour of the ISI framework, this is the opening paragraph from a 2013 report on a very successful preparatory school. In the style of Blink, much is captured in just one paragraph of 180 words. What else is there to say?

St John's College School is extremely successful in meeting its aims and gives its pupils a flying start to their education. It discovers and nurtures the gifts, talents and strengths of all pupils and supports their particular needs, so that they develop as well-rounded, well-balanced individuals who are able to shine in their chosen fields. Pupils' achievement from the EYFS onwards is exceptional, because they are given so many opportunities to succeed in so many areas. Their academic attainment is excellent, with the result that they are able to gain places and awards at prestigious selective senior schools. Many make excellent progress, particularly those pupils with SEND, because of the outstanding support they receive. Teaching is excellent, and boys and girls of all ages are enthusiastic, inquisitive and self-motivated learners because of this. Teachers have outstandingly good relationships with their pupils, and are often inspirational in their approach, firing up pupils' thirst for learning and fostering independent and co-operative learning skills. The curriculum and extra-curricular opportunities are excellent, offering pupils outstanding opportunities to use their skills and knowledge across a breadth of subjects.

Leading inspections

I wrote in Chapter 3 (page 21) about the restless school seeking to 'climb inside the inspector's skin' so as to prepare effectively for an external inspection. In echoing those thoughts, it does seem to me vital that school leaders seize the initiative with school inspections. They are high stakes. In some jurisdictions, school fees can be raised by school owners if the inspection outcomes improve on a previous best. In others, schools judged excellent or outstanding can assume certain wider responsibilities in supporting other schools and training teachers, thereby attracting considerable extra resources for their students. There is much to play for.

Inspection handbooks in different jurisdictions stipulate what inspectors expect to see by way of documentation, and they tend to cover similar territory: pupil progress data; school improvement plans; professional development records; minutes of meetings; safeguarding arrangements; school board/governors' minutes, etc.

I commend to schools preparing a 'less is more' or 'at a glance' file which leads inspectors helpfully to the key aspects of the school's provision and outcomes. Schools might take the following and shape their own accordingly.

'Less is More': file linked to September 2013 Ofsted inspection framework

A file that *leads* the inspection by including some key documents which (a) show the inspectors the SLT knows its school and (b) makes it easy for the inspectors. Think of them grappling for evidence under pressure in the inspection base – and they can reach for this file to solve their problems! *Climb inside the inspector's skin....*

1. Side-of-A4 personal statement about 'the school's story' from the head, demonstrating sustained capacity to improve at *all* levels. What has the school done to act on/improve previously identified (last Ofsted report) key issues? What are you doing to develop middle leadership? Succession planning, and support for other schools?

2. Short SEF, in whatever format the school judges – probably no more than four to six sides. Perhaps include a page on reading/ literacy/communication which acts as a guide to inspectors about where to see the school's best practice, from guided reading to one-to-one interventions to literacy across the secondary curriculum. (*Does the school's website celebrate what the school is good at?*)

3. Detail of all the classes: who is teaching and supporting; numbers of children (boys/girls) in each; G & T/EAL/SEN details. Ofsted's current preoccupations: SEND; able pupils; pupil premium and *target groups*; spending on sport. Case studies. Help inspectors with *identifying* pupils when you do joint observations.

4. Head's summary/spreadsheet of quality of teaching and learning – include current/recent observation schedule to assure inspectors that teachers are observed, and challenge/ support is followed up. Show you *know* your teachers: signpost performance management information, related to salary progression.

5. Note that the Ofsted inspection handbook reads: 'Inspectors should consider the extent to which the 'Teachers' Standards' are being met.' Make sure all teachers and support staff know the contents.

6. Four or five key pages from Raiseonline – annotated – which

tell the 'pupils' progress story' – and the key questions about *groups* of pupils that the school has asked itself and acted upon. (Link to separate, very well laid out data file!)

7. Key summary pages from school improvement/development plan: what is *this* school focusing upon? What's been the impact? Where is the school on its journey to good, from good to outstanding, etc?

8. Summary of recent pupil and parent questionnaires; school council minutes; minutes of TA meetings; safeguarding file/ SCR. Does Parent View say anything?

9. Latest governors' report – key pages which show the head and governors are communicating effectively. I ask for the first one of the academic year to see how the head has presented test and examination results? Can I, as a lay governor, understand what the head is telling me? Is the analysis clear to me as a lay person? Do I understand how this school is performing relative to local and national picture? *Renewed focus on governors in 2013 framework.*

10. Any papers which highlight the really distinctive and interesting aspects of the school – eg music and maths curriculum; SMSC dimensions; work with EAL parents; extra-curricular provision, etc. 'Thirst for knowledge' – a key phrase.

11. The final Ofsted report will leave the school with recommendations for improvement (see Ofsted house-style of bullet points) – almost write these for the inspector to show *you* know the school so well. Keep up your sleeve for the end of first day meeting with inspectors: Good/Outstanding/RI – *lead* the judgement.

How else can schools *lead* inspections rather than *be led*, perhaps feeling they are caught in the inspectors' bright headlights? My judgement is that the faltering, careless school (Chapter 10) is more than prone to those blinding lights.

Senior leaders in schools can prepare effectively for inspection by doing just a few things very well:

- Ensure everyone in the school understands the key aspects of the inspection framework, and the criteria against which the school is to be judged. It is vital for staff to know the language (the verbs, the adverbs, the adjectives) of the grade descriptors which inspectors are using.

- Brief all staff about the *process* of the inspection, whether teachers, support or administrative staff. Encourage teachers to seek feedback each time they are observed teaching; middle and senior leaders may be participating in the feedback. Brief school governors on the questions they can expect from inspectors.

- Expect all staff to have classrooms which 'sparkle' and exude a passion about learning; clear any clutter. A short file on pupils' attainment and progress should be readily available for a visiting inspector, alongside just a sample of well marked pupils' work. All marking must be up to date. And ensure a label on every door to identify which class it is.

- Set aside a comfortable room in which inspectors can work, with the clearly labelled documentation which has been requested. (Don't overload inspectors with documents!) For larger schools and thus larger inspections teams, a file for each inspector with key information: staff names, timetables, map of the school, timings of the day, etc. Make absolutely sure that the timetables covering the days the inspectors are in school are accurate. Attention to detail matters.

- Encourage staff to show inspectors the school and the pupils at their best. Good lead inspectors will, at an initial staff meeting, seek to put staff at their ease and encourage them to be open with the inspection team. Within time constraints, make sure staff show inspectors where very good practice exists.

- Ensure that those in the school who have a commanding knowledge of pupils' progress and attainment data have time and space, early in the inspection, to sit down with inspectors to present the evidence-based narrative. Lead inspectors will welcome clarity and a 'less is more' approach. Staff should be very well prepared to lead these discussions, and to secure further relevant data, if requested.

- Prepare middle and senior leaders to talk authoritatively about their roles, their responsibilities and, critically, their accountabilities. Leaders at all levels must be able to show inspectors, for example, the impact of their monitoring and tracking of pupils' progress or the impact of training they have led on classroom practice. Prepare a brief set of focused notes for any interview, with everyone knowing well what the school's currently identified points for development are.

- Know very well your own school's performance in the round, and be able to debate authoritatively with an inspection team, steering inspectors to particular evidence if you feel they have not scrutinised it sufficiently. Leaders should be in a position to write the summary findings and points for improvement, before the lead inspector does. For the effective leader, there should be no surprises.

- Be highly visible around the school throughout the inspection. Act positively and professionally at all times with the inspection team, modelling that behaviour for staff to follow. Lead inspectors will respond in kind.

- Seize the opportunity to thank staff and students for their work, as soon as the inspection is completed. Use the inspection report within and beyond the school to (a) celebrate what has been achieved and (b) set out future ambitions for sustaining success.

From a headteacher's perspective, an inspection feels successful if justice has been done to the school, if the head and staff have led the inspectors to the right places in order that they may make robust, well evidenced, independent judgements.

From the lead inspector's viewpoint, the hallmark of very good inspections is to be able to capture a particular school's story wisely and trenchantly in a final written report - to produce a narrative which the school recognises as describing accurately where it is and what it is doing at the point of inspection. Further, the inspection team will have, through constructive dialogue, identified the particular strengths and growth points of the school community.

In the same way that good schools manifest consistency, so too must the inspection team: consistent in applying inspection protocols; consistent in interpreting the framework's words and spirit; consistent in communicating effectively with pupils and staff; and leaving all involved at the school feeling personally and professionally enriched by the team's work.

In a chapter on inspection, it is perhaps appropriate for the last word to be left to a distinguished Senior Chief Inspector. These are the finely judged words of Sir Martin Roseveare from the 1950s, warm advice given to new HMI before they ventured into schools. May inspectors around the world read, learn and inwardly digest his wisdom. And, if I may say to colleague inspectors, don't go into a school unless you leave them feeling better for your having been there, however easy or tough your message.

'I am sure you will always remember that courtesy, consideration for others, evenness of temper and sincerity will be expected of you at all times.

You should always remember that when you visit a school it is an everyday affair for you, but an unusual and important occasion for the school.

Be a patient and sympathetic listener.'

Chapter 10

Why schools falter

Here is Edward Bear, coming downstairs now, bump, bump, bump, on the back of his head, behind Christopher Robin. It is, as far as he knows, the only way of coming downstairs, but sometimes he feels that there really is another way, if only he could stop bumping for a moment and think of it. And then he feels that perhaps there isn't.

Winnie-the-Pooh, A.A. Milne

A school journey

Try to tell a contemporary audience of new London teachers, as I have in a number of lectures, what it was like to be a teacher in one of the capital's comprehensives in the 1970s, and they simply don't believe the narrative. The past is a foreign country: they do things differently there. We certainly did.

The combination of teacher shortages, militant union action, members' ideological interferences, and a sprawling bureaucracy covering the inner London area led to some of the larger comprehensives simply being ungovernable. I know first-hand of one headteacher appointed to a secondary school, only to decline the position within a week of the start of the autumn term, frightened off by local union reps. (I was to experience similar myself on interview in Liverpool in 1985, the city then under leader Derek Hatton's illegal budget-setting regime.)

It was undeniably the case that union action for teachers' improved conditions of service led to part-time schooling, week in and week out, for many secondary students. It wasn't long before their classroom and corridor behaviour reflected that disaffection. As a young teacher I never quite forgave the antics of a striking few who pitched themselves against headteachers and the sensible day-to-day workings of a school.

Suffice to say, academic standards in many of those once flagship comprehensives – many with over 2000 students – were not what they should have been, despite the best endeavours of hard working staff; and let the considerable educational innovation of the time not be forgotten. Schools in major cities around the country suffered a similar though not as acute fate, while the shires were much less blighted. The demise of the Inner London Education Authority (ILEA) in 1990 marked the end of what some commentators have described as two lost and sad decades in the capital city's schools.

***

I next met school failure full on when I joined the highly respected school improvement division (SID) within Her Majesty's Inspectorate – and a better inspection training ground you would be pushed to find. For three years I travelled up and down the country inspecting and monitoring special, primary and secondary schools which, for one reason or another, had fallen on hard times - some to the point of desperation.

What did I encounter in these schools where educational dry-rot had been allowed to spread? Chronic lack of ambition by teachers, leaders and governors; benign neglect from local authorities; stubborn leaders who kept at bay anyone from the outside trying to help; dirty and unloved premises; careless relationships between staff and students; school systems operating for the convenience of the staff not the pupils; dysfunctional support staff; a culture of blame and denial – not all of these all of the time, but each school had a cocktail which included some of these pivotal factors.

First and second monitoring visits to these schools were frequently dispiriting. Hard conversations were the norm. As an inspector you aimed of course to make yourself redundant: to help accelerate the school's journey of self-improvement; to share in the school's eventual successes; to see pupils, teachers and leaders regain self-esteem and pride in their place of work. It does not surprise me at all that I have stayed in personal and professional contact with most of the headteachers who led those improvement journeys for their school communities.

They taught me so much in such a short space of time. I salute them.

***

Completing my trinity of experiences in, let us say, schools on their uppers, has taken me in recent years to different parts of the world, in the role of helping to establish new national and local inspection systems. It would be unfair to identify specific locations here, because I visited schools at the behest of local administrators wanting assistance with how their schools could be improved.

Interestingly, whilst the cocktail of dysfunction mirrored to some extent what I was familiar with in England, other very different factors came into play, sometimes reflecting the relative 'youth' of a schooling system. Significant among these factors: no teachers; poorly trained teachers; teachers who were not paid on time and therefore did not turn up for work; temporary leaders; inadequate classroom resources; overcrowded, unlit classrooms; complete absence of line management and accountability – yet, almost always, students hungry to learn.

***

Boswell: 'Then sir, what is poetry?'

Johnson: 'Why sir, it is much easier to say what it is not. We all know what light is; but it is not easy to tell what it is.'

The Life of Dr. Johnson

'Failure' can be an alarming word: heart failure; aircraft engine failure; train signal failure. Suffice to say, for those few schools which are not serving their children with a dignified and proper education, I think the word is appropriate. I know what failure in schools – home and abroad – looks, feels and smells like. As someone who has reviewed and inspected over 800 schools, I can recognise it pretty quickly.

Do failure and dysfunction happen because of conspiracy, cock-up, or benign neglect? Rarely in my experience is failure wilful. It can be through ignorance in the Latin sense of the word *ignoscere* – not knowing. It can be for some or all of the many factors I've listed above, and is often complex to untangle. It is rare for good schools with well embedded systems to decline badly, though not unknown. Sometimes an extreme event in a local community can damage a school's reputation irretrievably.

Overall, it would be fair to say – certainly in England – that the number of what the Department for Education (DfE) would describe as failing schools has been reduced to a real minimum – and still the work goes on in those urban and shire pockets to eradicate inadequate educational provision.

The careless school

'Given a choice between changing and proving that it is not necessary, most people get busy with the proof.'

J.K. Galbraith

There remain too many schools which just bob along, never really breaking through to being thriving and confident schools. They survive and falter, rather than flourish. They never quite reach that 'tipping point' which leads to sustaining success. When ill winds blow, they rush to build walls rather than windmills. They dig deep in their routines to find reasons not to change. Might we reasonably describe these as *careless* rather than *careful* schools? Picking up the title of this book, might it be fair to suggest that those who lead and teach in these schools are not *restless* enough, are inward-facing and all too content with a dull status quo?

The careless school – if that is not too unkind a term – may historically feature some of the following leadership characteristics: headteachers who have allowed themselves to take their eyes off leading learning and instead been drawn into the role of social carers; leaders who have become too concerned with compliance and thus risk-averse; governing bodies and school boards which have just not challenged sufficiently.

Henry Ford's famous dictum – 'Whether you think that you can, or that you can't, you are usually right' – might well be apt in these contexts. Almost always, what is required is a fundamental *cultural shift* across the school. Mixing metaphors: (a) The right people need to be on the bus (the wrong people off it), and they need to know which seat to sit in; (b) It is not about teaching old dogs new tricks. Old dogs need to *unlearn* their old tricks.

Does this following description characterise or caricature their daily routines?

Teamwork

There are four people named Everybody, Somebody, Anybody and Nobody. There was an important job to be done and Everybody was asked to do it. Everybody was sure Somebody would do it. Anybody could have done it, but Nobody did it.

Somebody got angry about that, because it was Everybody's job. Everybody thought Anybody could do it but Nobody realised that Everybody wouldn't do it. It ended up that Everybody blamed Somebody when Nobody did what Anybody could have done.'

So what's to be done?

What needs to happen *differently* to effect lasting change in these faltering schools, in the best interests of pupils and staff? In establishing a brand new school and learning centre in Milton Keynes in 1999, I worked with a superb founding team of staff and governors. From his considerable international experience in environmental matters, the chair of governors Chris Pym insisted we spent a development day on 'how projects fail'. We rehearsed in particular the *unintended consequences* of our extensive plans. (I commend such an exercise to any group of school leaders initiating change.)

For schools which have faltered and stumbled along, these are not blank canvases, and that has to be borne in mind in leading cultural shifts. In each case, 'tipping points' will be reached and need to be seized.

So proceeding with the caution of unintended consequences, let's take the faltering school. Let us give it a tried and tested 'less is more' blueprint for school self-improvement: seven platforms upon which to base future success.

Seven Platforms

Platform 1: Expectations

Establishing whole-school high expectations is the starting point for any improvement journey. This starts with those who own, govern and lead the school. Context matters, so a locally determined set of 'non-negotiables' must be agreed by all those who work and study within the particular school community. An agreed set of 'living values' underpins a healthy organisation. *Consistency* of expectations in classrooms, corridors, recreational spaces, staffroom and offices is a watchword. Systems are adhered to. Collusion with any unsatisfactory practice is unacceptable, at any time. Sameness is the enemy of good; individuality and difference should be valued.

Platform 2: Behaviours

The behaviours of staff, students and families towards one another and the school must at all times be proper. Young and old, male and female alike are treated with dignity. Clear examples of best behaviours and attitudes are modelled consistently and shared. There is no shouting or 'dark sarcasm of the classroom'. There is laughter and kindness. From the moment anyone comes through the school gate they know which kinds of behaviour are acceptable, and those which are not. Staff are expected to be professionally *friendly* towards one another, but not *friends* who bring into school issues which should be left at the school-gate. A professional working environment permeates.

Platform 3: Environments

School environments shape lives and determine staff and students' daily well-being. Owners, governors and leaders must establish consistently safe, clean and engaging learning environments, from classrooms to corridors to playgrounds to the wider campus. If the tiniest piece of glass is cracked or graffiti appears, prompt action for renewal must be taken. The right temperature and degree of light for high quality learning should be the norm. Dining facilities, library spaces, staff workrooms, staff and student common rooms – attention to detail in these spaces lifts morale and the 'can-do' spirit of everyone. Create an environment – every nook and cranny – which lifts the spirits, and everyone's attendance rates will rise.

Platform 4: Teachers

Teachers determine pupils' outcomes; no school can be better than the quality of its teachers. The recruitment and retention of high quality teachers is fundamental. The creation of a cadre of colleagues who promote a love of learning, scholarship and creativity amongst their pupils is well on the way to producing a good school. Teachers must know their subjects and shape a vibrant curriculum. Investment in their professional development is a critical aspect of a school which is intent on building success. All teachers should be well educated and well read. Where teachers require an update in their skills and knowledge, the school must provide proper support, and hold teachers to account. Above all, the teaching staff must have challenging ambitions for all children that they can attain high outcomes, academically and socially.

Platform 5: Supporters

'Supporters' are many and varied in the school context. In-class support staff are expected to make a significant contribution to pupils' learning and progress; their professional development is as vital as that provided for teachers. School administrators create ways of doing which ensure day-to-day organisation is consistently smooth and 'can-do'. Families are actively engaged in their children's learning, and communication with them is first-class. Governors play a vital part in keeping the school on its toes, regularly and without flinching from difficult decisions. The skills of key community partners are harnessed for students' well-being and readiness for transition to the next phase of their education.

Platform 6: Leaders

Think of children and young people first as leaders: harness their distinctive knowledge to shape the school's present and future successes. All staff should be aware that 'leadership' in one guise or another is expected of them and that the school believes in growing its own leadership teams. Current and potential middle and senior leaders need strong professional support and development, and clear lines of accountability. They need to see the enjoyment, fun and job satisfaction there is to be had in a leadership position. Headteachers remain decisive in moving a school forwards at pace, ambitious for success, restless to improve. They need to take the right advice, and ignore the wrong advice. They need to recognise and seize the 'tipping points'. They need to judge when fierce and fearless leadership is required. Headteachers must demonstrate that it's a great job to lead a school.

Platform 7: Critics

On a journey of school improvement, there will be welcome and unwelcome critics. Leaders need to see their school from time to time through the eyes of the complaining customer. Interpret and harness that complaint well, and fewer complaints will come in the future. Schools need to be unrelenting in how they manage community perceptions of what they are doing. Reputations are hard won and too easily lost. The increasingly successful school regularly welcomes candid friends to visit and report on what is going well and what still needs improvement. It certainly has no qualms about *leading* a passing inspection team to catch staff and students at their best.

Coda

The Seven Platforms will, in the right hands, move the school to be securely good, thriving on local community confidence. What then? As one international school headteacher I know expresses it, *excellence* is a next step for those who:

- care more than others think is wise
- risk more than others think is safe
- dream more than others think is practical
- expect more than others think is possible.

Chapter 11

Excellence as Standard

We are what we repeatedly do. Excellence, then, is not an act, but a habit.

Aristotle

The standard operation

The American political scientist Francis Fukuyama in his seminal work *The End of History and the Last Man* (1992) argued that the world-wide spread of liberal democracies marked the end point of humanity's social evolution. In essence, Fukuyama contested that the final form of government had arrived. Is there a similar sense in which we know today what we need to know about creating great schools? A thread running through this book has certainly been to suggest that in large measure we do.

Widely shared across the world is that great *school systems* deploy globally benchmarked standards and see the effective use of data and sharp accountability as key to success. These systems can demonstrate that 'no child is left behind'. There is significant investment in recruiting great people to teach and in their training and development over time. In turn, great leaders are grown who are able to lead, manage and change local educational communities to be outstanding in performance. That's the virtuous and, many would contest, the proven narrative.

As to great *schools*, international educators would argue that the following key ingredients make up the professional cocktail: schools excel at what they do in a consistent manner; they have strong values and high expectations; their achievements do not happen by chance but through highly reflective, carefully planned strategies; there is a high degree of internal consistency; leadership is well distributed and ambitious to move the school forward.

But let me move beyond the researchers' well-grounded findings and beyond the inspectors' lexicon of judging schools to be poor, satisfactory, good or outstanding. My contention here is that what needs to emerge across school systems is, to borrow from the medical profession, 'the standard operation'. As a patient entering an established hospital for an appendectomy, a hip replacement, or a kidney transplant – operations of increasing complexity – wherever in the world we are, doctors will swing into action with the standard operation. Barring complications and assuming competent physicians, the patient will leave hospital with a body refreshed.

Before the reader responds in thought with examples of flawed operations let me at once – in the tradition of best teaching – indulge in a purposeful digression. For a number of years I chaired tribunals for the Thames Valley Health Authority, investigating alleged medical malpractice. In concluding these tribunals, without exception, patients wanted (a) an apology; (b) an explanation as to what had happened in the treatment process; (c) a reassurance from those in charge that future patients would not suffer similarly.

Yes, mistakes in the standard operation do happen, but very rarely are they wilful. If you read no other account on this subject, and of what it is to be a leading surgeon and public servant, then read Henry Marsh's *Do No Harm: Stories of Life, Death and Brain Surgery*. Having personally experienced both the following medical trauma, I was tickled by his own tale of being struck by a retina detachment and then, partially sighted, falling downstairs and breaking a leg. This led to his first experience, aged 56, of a sleepless night in an NHS hospital ward!

That is all on the lighter side. When he turns to his work proper, the narrative is utterly compelling:

I often have to cut into the brain and it is something I hate doing. With a pair of diathermy forceps I coagulate the beautiful and intricate red blood vessels that lie on the brain's shining surface. I cut into it with a small scalpel and make a hole through which I push with a fine sucker. The idea that my sucker is moving through thought itself, though emotion and reason, that memories, dreams and reflections should consist of jelly, is simply too strange to understand. All I can see in front of me is matter. Yet I know if I stray into the wrong area, into what neurosurgeons call eloquent brain, I will be faced by a damaged and disabled patient when I go round to the recovery ward.

Brain surgery is dangerous, and modern technology has only reduced the risk to a certain extent. Much of what happens in hospitals is a matter of luck, both good and bad; success and failure are often out of the doctor's control.

Henry Marsh

Excellence as standard for schools

Much of this book has focused on teachers and leaders. But what about schools from the consumers' viewpoint? What might 'the standard operation' look like, wherever in the world you are? We might reasonably expect, in a wealthy and highly developed society, that what I'll title as *Excellence as Standard* would be the norm for a school. I shall try to describe its features.

'The bearer of these presents is Michelangelo, the Sculptor. His nature is such that he has to be drawn out by kindness and encouragement, but if he be treated well, and love be shown to him, he will accomplish things that will make the whole world wonder.'

Michelangelo's testimonial to the Pope

Schools are a people business. The inner belief and commitment to realising excellence by those who lead schools is *the* starting point. At its beating heart the excellent school *is* a place where people care more than others think is wise, risk more than others think is safe, dream more than others think is practical, and expect more than others think is possible.

The following is an extract from a thoughtfully worded advertisement for new employees to join a five-star international hotel and restaurant:

'The type of person we are looking for can demonstrate:

- A desire to improve themselves in terms of skills, knowledge and experience
- Good organizational skills and high service standards
- Patience, a sense of humour and an ability to accept and act on constructive feedback
- An ability to work on their own initiative and also to be a good team player
- Excellent and pro-active communication skills
- An eye for detail and a willingness to improve all aspects of the service we offer
- A positive attitude to all aspects of the job including enthusiasm, a professional and common sense approach and a dedication to the interests of the business.'

The excellent school sets out its stall to employ such people in the same way that any five-star business does. The particular skills and knowledge required of a teacher are non-negotiable; so are attitudes, dispositions and high service standards.

The excellent school is a first choice for families, and an employer of first choice for staff. Academic standards reflect the fact that, whatever their starting points, children and young people make very good progress through their school years, and achieve as well as they can in public examinations. Children feel good about themselves within the school; their talents and gifts – whatever they may be – are spotted and nourished. The wider community wants to be associated with the school's successes.

The environment which children enter each day is attractive, light, clean, safe and welcoming; young children run into the playground at the start of the day, with barely a glimpse back to their parent. Older children arrive in good time at the start of the school day and stay on at the end, perhaps to sit in the library or café area. Physical space – and care for that space – matters.

Throughout the school day there is a sense of calm and purpose, because staff have clear expectations about behaviour and attitudes to learning. There is very little 'white noise' to distract staff and students going about their business. Day-to-day organisation is unfussy. No one complicates matters. The school resists passing educational fads and fashions, confident in its tried and tested practices for the community of learners it serves.

Time is well used. The curriculum and lessons motivate the children, as does the co-curricular programme of sports, drama, arts and music. Students produce work and create performances which are of *real* quality, whether in the sciences, the humanities or the arts. They ask deep questions of themselves, take risks in their learning and develop collaborative skills. Students make a difference every day, whether in their own unique progress or to the work and well-being of others and the school community. Each child is valued and understood as an individual: academically, intellectually, socially, emotionally, and as a spiritual being. Staff recognise the profound importance of childhood as captured in J.M. Barrie's words from *Peter Pan*:

'On these magic shores children at play are for ever beaching their coracles. We too have been there; we can still hear the sound of the surf, though we shall land no more'.

Those who lead the school are optimistic, approachable and in clear, quiet command. Their craftsmanship, if you like, is of great simplicity and strength. Their instincts and intuitions are always asking what they can do to make the school better. And if they are 'trail blazing' in the external educational world, they never forget that tweaking and revising everyday matters in the school corridors and hallways is vital. Leaders ensure that staff are well looked after pastorally and professionally, so that a trademark of the school is staff continuity. Staff know at all times that they are servants of the school. Those who leave do so for good reason and are warmly thanked and recognised by parents, children and governors for their significant contributions to the school community.

An excellent school is high performing in all aspects of its life and work. It has a distinctive impact on children's and young people's lives. Attention to detail matters. Staff will always go that extra mile to ensure an upset child is cared for, or best prepared for an interview or examination. Staff believe almost anything is possible: whatever the barrier a child may present, excellent schools find a way through. Decisions are made in the best interests of the child, not the staff. And look behind the front-desk for just a moment: the school telephone is answered promptly and courteously; the school nurse rota is clear to students; someone is checking carefully the grammar of the school newsletter.

Excellence as Standard in schools is about an embedded culture of thinking and doing. Those leading and teaching in the school do care, risk, dream and expect more than others think is possible. They do so every day the school is open, and as much again in holiday periods. They have a passion to be the best they can be. They strive to be expert in as many ways as they can be, in nurturing young people's talents and aspirations, not some or most of the time, but *all* of the time. The quest for excellence becomes their habit and their purposeful practice.

One important qualifying note should be added to this notion of *Excellence as Standard*. Excellent schools vary in size, tradition, age-range, denomination, context, location and many other characteristics: each school's unique culture brings an added and vital dimension to its overall achievements and mission. Each school is excellent in generically similar and individually distinctive ways. Practices vary, but processes are steeped in the same five-star mould. Consistency yes, sameness no.

***

In many aspects of our daily lives, notably with regard to the provision of core services in the community, we want excellence to meet our aspirations. Naturally we each have slightly different interpretations of what high quality means. *Excellence as Standard* as set out above could of course be codified, but that's what auditors do with relish and a particular purpose in mind.

Earlier in the book I quoted the teacher and social historian R.H. Tawney: 'What a wise parent would wish for their children, so the state must wish for all its children'. In the same way that the standard operation in hospital is a manifestation of the best medicine which can be offered to the patient, *Excellence as Standard* can become an equivalent kite-mark in our global schooling systems, today and for tomorrow. It is what parents and nations alike want for their children.

An excellent school (and an excellent school system) delivers superior performance and has a high impact over a sustained period of time.

Expectations rise ineluctably – that is the human condition, that is the global imperative. Echoing F. Scott Fitzgerald from my opening pages, definitions and descriptions of excellence in schools will not remain static, they will forever be boats beating on against the currents, 'borne back ceaselessly into the past.'

te Leadership

A celebr   once tactlessly asked, after a famous victory, if it hadn't   econd-in-command.

The gen........   e before answering: 'Maybe so. But one thing is certain. If the battle had been lost, I would have lost it'.

There are probably as many pages written on the subject of leadership as there are leaders. Included amongst the catchiest titles I've come across are: *Why should anyone be led by you?*, *What got you here won't get you there*, *The Art of Seduction*, *Call Me Ted*, *Leaders Eat Last*, and *Polar Bear Pirates*. And a quick scroll through the Amazon bookshop will uncover another dozen in similar vein.

There may be one or two articles and books on school leadership which have had a particular influence upon you – recommended by a colleague or friend, by someone whose own style of leadership you admire, by a motivational speaker, or perhaps by someone who has taught you.

In putting together this chapter I not only call to mind the words of Goethe quoted on page 7, but those too of a Chief Rabbi who wryly observed: 'Everything has been said before, though not everyone has yet said it'.

The chapter is written in two parts: Part A distils my own reflections on school leadership. Part B lists some pithy advice from the famous and infamous.

Part A: Two Minute Leadership

I vividly recall, as a deputy head, being told by my headteacher that I would not make the mistakes I was watching him make – but that I should proceed with my career in the certain knowledge that I would make my own. His advice was perspicacious.

Leaders are primates and human, prone to wise judgement and crass error in equal measure. There is just no stopping it. But there is something to be learned from observing others, both what they do successfully and where they falter. In that spirit, and in the spirit of those one-minute-manager and one-minute-father books you find in any airport bookshop, the following are offered. Rooted in various encounters, they are not presented in any order of importance, rather as a series of take-away moments. Space has been left at the end of the list for you to add your own, to pass on to those with whom you work and who are busy noting your mistakes …

- *Talk with and listen to the students* – they help you keep your finger on the school's pulse, its corridor rumour and playground gossip. Walk through classrooms every day you can, even if it's just to say 'hello'.

- *Know your community* – if it is changing, respond promptly. Don't wait to be told that the number of bilingual learners has doubled since you last walked the corridors.

- *Compliment someone at least once a day* – you may find it hard to include all your staff here, but try. Practise on someone who might least expect the smile from you. Offer to take a lesson for them. And remember: cynics don't only grow old, they die.

- *Be resilient in the face of failure* – admit when you're wrong. When you apologise, never add 'but' to the end of the apology or you'll gain a reputation for insincerity.

- *Grasp nettles tightly* – then they won't hurt. Remember Aesop? Spot the member of staff who has retired, but hasn't told you yet.

- *Remember Bertrand Russell* – 'the trouble with the world is that the stupid are cocksure and the intelligent are full of doubt'.

- *Invest in high quality toilets for students* – you won't regret explaining that additional expenditure to the governors. They have children at the school, and will have been told about the plush soap dispensers, luxuriant plants and framed mirrors in the loos.

- *Invest in classrooms* – teachers and students spend 1500 hours a year in them. Buy a chaise longue, Nespresso machine, iPad and water cooler for every teacher.

- *Abolish bells* – they belong in another era. Put plants and carpets across the curriculum. Install a luxury fish tank in the entrance foyer to calm irate parents.

- *Your best friends are the dustbin and the delete button* – so much 'stuff' comes your way, so protect others from it. Cut bureaucracy for your colleagues. De-clutter classrooms, offices and staffroom – secure a deal with a skip company.

- *Less is more* – be concise. Remember the following: the Lord's Prayer – 54 words. The Ten Commandments – 297 words. The American Declaration of Independence – 300 words. The EEC Directive for exporting duck eggs – 26,911 words.

- *Bottle the teachers who are young at heart* – infect everyone with their talents. Ensure a variety of skills and intelligences in staff you appoint. Grow your own great people. Certainly look to recruit people who are brighter than you are.

- *Stick close to your values* – and be occasionally sceptical of them. Be explicit about the ethical principles upon which you lead.

- *Have confidence in your moral commitment, instinct and intuitions –* and have someone to restrain you, probably matron or the groundsman.

- *Enjoy confronting authority and taking risks –* practise the Jesuit principle of management, namely that it's easier to beg forgiveness than seek permission. Say 'no' to a directive and that you believe instead in phyletic gradualism.

- *Thrive on accountability –* and occasional chaos. Remember the old maxim (misquoting Kipling) that if you have kept your head when everyone around you is losing theirs, you probably haven't quite understood what's going on.

- *Keep in mind the big picture –* someone has to. Remember the 'third eye' – challenge orthodoxies even if you then find out why some things are orthodox; it's worth the journey.

- *Communicate, communicate, communicate –* and time the communications well. Timing is all. If colleagues disagree with you, they'll say you haven't been communicating properly. *How* you say something is as important as *what* you say.

- *Tell good stories –* people remember them. Stories define who you are in the minds of others, for better or worse. Humour works, not sarcasm.

- *Avoid delusions of grandeur –* for everyone's sake, be reasonably predictable. Perception is all. You're paid handsomely to smile. And be a great teacher!

- *Don't assume rationality on the part of the people you are dealing with –* accept the idea that there are multiple perceptions of every situation. Learn to live with shades of grey.

- *Spare a thought for Bloom –* knowledge, comprehension, application, analysis, evaluation, synthesis. Not everyone is as capable as you pretend to be of moving upwards through Bloom's taxonomy of thinking. Some will get stuck half-way.

- *Pace yourself –* excellence is not an act but a habit. Focus on a limited number of objectives at a time. Secure a culture of co-workers, not hierarchies.

- *Read Seneca and the Stoics –* strive for moral and intellectual perfection. Get the staff to read widely. Be curious and find time for your own interests. Ditch the guilt.

- *Take Tuesdays off –* if you're going to take 'dedicated headteacher time' off-site, don't do it on a Friday or the staff will think you're off to the ski slopes for the weekend. Learn to develop your inner sloth. Rest your heartbeat somehow.

- Add your own...

***

Part B: Leaders' Rules

Taken from a catholic range of sources, the following may or may not offer some resonance and wise advice. Is there something about the number eight?

Nelson Mandela: Eight lessons of leadership (Madiba's rules)

1. Courage is not the absence of fear – it's inspiring others to move beyond it
2. Lead from the front – but don't leave your base behind
3. Lead from the back – and let others believe they are in front
4. Know your enemy – and learn about his favourite sport
5. Keep your friends close – and your rivals even closer
6. Appearances matter – and remember to smile
7. Nothing is black or white
8. Quitting is leading too.

Eight leadership lessons from the world's most powerful women

1. Stay determined
2. Be courageous
3. Think bigger
4. Take calculated risks
5. Remain disciplined
6. Hire smart
7. Manage your career
8. Delegate at work and at home.

Michael Bloomberg, former mayor of New York: 'High fives'

1. Hire the best – and give them room to innovate
2. Do the hard things first
3. Leave the ideological battles and party politics to the national debaters Mayors are elected to be doers, not debaters
4. There is no Democratic or Republican way of cleaning the streets
5. Make accountability a trademark.

Sheryl Sandberg, CEO Facebook: Advice to future women leaders

1. Find something you love doing, and do it with gusto
2. Think big: close the ambition gap

3. Believe in yourself – lean in!
4. Leadership belongs to those who take it
5. Make the right choices, personally and professionally
6. Challenge yourself, or you'll get bored
7. Find a job that matters to you, and matters to others
8. What would you do if you weren't afraid?
9. Navigate the hard times.

Martin Luther King: Eight leadership lessons
1. Leaders do not sugar-coat reality
2. Leaders engage the heart
3. Leaders refuse to accept the status quo
4. Leaders create a sense of urgency
5. Leaders call people to act in accord with their highest values
6. Leaders refuse to settle
7. Leaders acknowledge the sacrifice of their followers
8. Leaders paint a vivid picture of a better tomorrow.

National Football League (NFL) Coach Dick Vermeil: Seven common sense principles of leadership
1. Make sure people know you care about them
2. Be a good example
3. Create an atmosphere that people enjoy working in
4. Define, delegate, then lead
5. Bring emotional and physical energy to the workplace
6. Build relationships as you implement your process, vision and value system
7. Establish credibility by being sincere, believable and trustworthy.

Chapter 13

Futures thinking

In the year 3535
Ain't gonna need to tell the truth, tell no lies
Everything you think, do and say
Is in the pill you took today

In the year 4545
Ain't gonna need your teeth, won't need your eyes
You won't find a thing to chew
Nobody's gonna look at you

In the Year 2525, Zager & Evans

Unchanged schools?

My school journey began in a Church of England primary school in Bath in 1957. We lived opposite the school in one of the handsome streets of Beau Nash's Georgian city; my parents rented a third-floor flat for 30 shillings a week, milk and coal included. The diurnal round of my primary class of 41 children was English, mathematics, painting, a little history and geography, and nature study in the adjacent Henrietta Park. Each Friday after a fish and chips school lunch (I can smell it now) we walked to St John's Church for a service of thanks.

I recently visited two village primaries in rural France – public and catholic sharing the same campus in the high Alps – and their daily routines have in truth changed little down the generations, though skiing for the children on Fridays takes the place of my walk to church. One can travel through much of Europe finding the same, and through America and visit primary schoolrooms little different from those described by Harper Lee in that great American novel every English teenager has studied, *To Kill a Mockingbird*.

History is not traced in straight lines, but in jagged and discontinuous strokes. In many aspects of our lives there is imperceptible and incremental change; in others, the extraordinary becomes the commonplace at a faster and faster rate. We live longer, we travel further, standards of living rise, technological shift happens. Compare a hospital's ways of doings in 2014 with those they practised in 1957: they are very different as a result of the advances in medical sciences. Yet compare a school between the same two dates, and apart from the demise of the blackboard, teachers' salaries having risen and class sizes reduced, what differences do you notice? Read again on page 27 that enchanting description of Beachamwell, dated 1977. Children will be children.

Perhaps I exaggerate a little: to make a point about schools being a vital part of a society's past, present and future, blending tradition and change ever so carefully in order to preserve formative cultural values. If I look in a little more depth from the 1950s to today, what of significance has *arrived* in the English school system and in schools?

- Abolition of the 11+ (in most parts of the country)
- Phasing out of technical and secondary modern schools
- Comprehensive schools
- Academies
- National Curriculum
- GCSEs replaced O levels
- Local Management of Schools
- Teachers' performance management
- National Professional Qualification for Headteachers
- League tables and pupil performance data
- Ofsted and published reports on schools
- Investment in teaching assistants
- A range of technological devices in classrooms
- Higher Education fees.

What might you add to the list?

Already in a 'list of significance' such as this, one immediately observes that some aspects may not be here to stay – shift happens. And, worth noting, the gold standard of A level, strongly backed by UK universities, has remained.

Possible, probable and preferable futures

Environmentalists are fond of shaping their thinking about the future into possible, probable and preferred scenarios. What no futures thinking can anticipate is the occasional seismic paradigm shift which a genius such as Pablo Piccaso, Martha Graham, Igor Stravinski, Bill Gates or Mahatma Ghandi brought to their different fields of influence. Who knows what that might be in the field of education in say 2030? Futurology is a mug's business, but fun and often instructive about both the present and the future. I have written enough policy advice for local and national leaders and politicians to know that it is *practice which shapes policy*, that way round.

William Gibson, sci-fi author of the influential 1984 novel *Necromancer*, observed cannily that the future is already here, but it's just not very evenly distributed. What is someone's practice today in a school, classroom, local authority or academy chain will emerge tomorrow as party policy and, if you are not careful, will become an orthodoxy. Educational practice is littered with them. (As I write in the spring of 2014, the major political parties are drafting their educational manifestos for May 2015, though it has to be said that education policies are rarely decisive ingredients at national elections.)

One of the most interesting developments in policy making in recent years has been influenced by the so-called 'Nudge theory', which argues that human behaviours are more readily influenced through indirect suggestion and positive reinforcement, rather than through forced compliance. Politicians may then think twice about rushing to legislate.

In aspects of UK society in recent years, this has been fascinating to watch: music playing at train stations to encourage people to skip up the stairs and increase their heart-rates; new driving licences issued with the default position that if a driver is killed in a crash, his organs will be donated; personalised text messages relating to late payments much more effective than final warning notices. The impact of the Behavioural Insights Team in Whitehall, which promotes Nudge, is not to be under-estimated. That balance of, and tension between, Nudge and Diktat will come to underpin 21st century policy making by future governments and leaders across the globe.

The schools system in 2030

To turn in practice to the future. Let me look at possible and probable futures in two parts. I shall assert matters confidently, to provoke. As reader, you can choose which you prefer, or think up your own.

2030. This is potentially just three Parliaments away. Whoever is in power, the entire period 2015-2030 will be dominated in policy terms by the expanding and ageing UK population. When Bismarck, in the 1880s, introduced into Germany his social insurance programmes, the pensionable age was set with the expectation that very few would reach it. In the 1940s our own William Beveridge was a little more generous in his planning. Today in the UK, the average life expectancy of a woman is 82.5 years and for a man 78.5 years. Politicians, on our behalf, are finding it predictably difficult to effect changes to the welfare state in its broadest reach.

Related to commentary in various chapters of *The Restless School*, I believe that educational policies and legislation will during the next three Parliaments:

1. Extend the provision, range and diversity of independent-state schools

2. Demand greater collaboration between publicly funded schools and independent, fee-paying schools. (Politicians have come to grasp that the not-so-secret success of long-standing independent schools is their *independence*.)

3. Focus relentlessly on social mobility and 'closing the achievement gap'

4. Capitalise on cultural diversity and an expanding school population, with school campuses open 24/7

5. Increase both schools' autonomy and schools' accountabilities; a common inspection system operating across *all* schools will be established

6. Experiment continuously with 'the middle tier' (what lies between London's Department for Education and 25,000 individual schools?) and the role of democratically elected local authorities

7. Tinker with the profession and training routes for teachers, with incremental improvement

8. Tinker with the curriculum and examination system, consistently benchmarked against international best, with variable success.

Two notes:

a. The 'third rail' of British politics during the 2015-2030 period will be the introduction of fee-paying health and education for all, and means-tested state pensions.

b. Walk into the foyer of the Department for Education in London, and there are photos of all the Secretaries of State for Education since Rab Butler and Ellen Wilkinson in the 1940s; what most of them have in common is their fewer than three-years tenure of office. Many distinguished and fine public servants among them, long-term planning is not in the nature of the office. In my school journey years, the current DfE has also been called: the Ministry of Education; Department of Education and Science; Department for Education; Department for Education and Employment; Department for Education and Skills; and Department for Children, Schools and Families. I do not guess here what other acronyms may befall it, prior to its complete abolition sometime in the late 2020s.

The schools system in 2064

Chapter 6 hypothesised on the future life of a child born in 2014 and the global context in which her schooling and working life will take place. I extend that vision here. The girl will celebrate her 50th birthday in 2064; tragic personal accident aside, she will be less than halfway through her normal life. She may by then have seen the disappearance of Belgium, blindness and Google, and the advent of artificial eyes, lunar universities and a single global currency.

In my lifetime the unthinkable has become the commonplace – especially in relation to the GRIN technologies: genetics, robotics, internet, nanotechnology. Over the next 50 years the world will witness regional and religious wars, devastating plagues and significant environmental degradation; but the human instinct to survive, be ingenious and fight back against any whiff of political, religious or technological totalitarianism will win through.

Humans will command machines, not the other way around as science fiction has led us to believe. Certainly we shall never see realised the dystopia envisioned in Henry Sleaser's compelling short story *Examination Day*. In the story, all 12 year-olds have to take an examination which decides their future. The narrative concludes, chillingly, with a phone call to the parents of Dickie Jordan.

'This is the Government Educational Service. Your son, Richard M Jordan, Classification 600 – 115, has completed the Government examination. We regret to inform you that his intelligence quotient is above the Government regulation, according to Rule 84, Section 5 of the New Code. You may specify by telephone whether you wish his body interred by the Government, or you would prefer a private burial place. The fee for Government burial is ten dollars.'

In the UK in **2064**, when the third largest 'country by population', after India and China, will be the people who live and work outside the country of their birth:

1. The government, public purse and general taxation will no longer fund schools or hospitals. All schools will be fee-paying, bringing them in line with the nursery and university sectors. The vigorous municipalism which created our hospitals, parks, and schools will no longer feature.

2. There will be little structural and organisational difference between schools across the globe: all will be *de facto* independent and international. All will operate *Excellence As Standard*, a common approach to school organisation and effective teaching and learning.

3. Most nations on earth will have established high quality compulsory education for girls and boys to age 24.

4. Schools around the world will follow a shared international curriculum and examination system, by way of entry for 80% of school students to higher education.

5. Schools will remain as agents of social control. They will operate year-round. There will be daily attendance at these institutions for younger children (0-15), with older students (aged 16-116) tele-working part-time, given the online curricula which they will be following. The de-schoolers will still not have won.

6. The noble profession of teaching will be held in the same high esteem in society as gene doctors. Teachers typically will enter the profession at 30 and teach, with varying career breaks, until 80.

7. The mega-cities of the world, from North America to Africa to Asia, will deliver a quality of education to their populations which will represent a significant step up from what we currently consider to

be excellent or outstanding, rooted in genetic engineering and nano-technology.

Coda: if I am right in asserting that the extraordinary becomes the commonplace, at a faster and faster rate, then much of the above will be in place by 2040.

***

The classroom of today and tomorrow

I was sitting in a regular Grade 8 class in the UAE. I looked round to see a united nations gathered in this international school. With the teacher's permission I asked Amir to write down the names and nationalities of the class. This he wrote, 'for Mr Roy':

Salman	*USA/UAE*	Sophia	*Australia*
Shahnawaz	*Pakistan*	Vlad	*Russia*
Babur	*Pakistan*	Amir	*Iran*
Alireza	*Canada/Iran/Russia*	Noora	*UAE*
Ayaka	*Japan*	Geungeong	*Korea*
Sondos	*Jordan*	Hetvi	*India*
Aaryan	*India/South Africa*	Tanya	*Canada/India*
Aiya	Iraq	Samer	*Lebanon*
Muhamad	*Egypt*	Ronald	*Hungary*
Wali	*Pakistan*	Zain	*South Africa*
Fahad	*Pakistan/UAE/USA*	Dinesh	*India/Hong Kong*
Alasri	*UAE*	Reem	*UAE/Saudi Arabia*
Ladina	*Switzerland*	Kayla	*South Africa*

Don't you just want to take this class to the United Nations building in New York, and affirm: the peoples of the world *can* lie down together peacefully!

***

Diving bells and butterflies

How shall we move our schooling system from 2014 to 2030 to 2064?

Teachers and school leaders *will* find practical and innovative solutions to building a golden bridge between teaching and learning practices that are past, passing and to come.

That will be the story of coming generations of educators. They should always hold dear to the 'third eye', that eye which challenges orthodoxies in the best interests of students. They should also take inspiration from that extraordinarily powerful memoir *The Diving Bell and the Butterfly* by Jean-Dominique Bauby in which a distinguished magazine editor falls into a coma and emerges from it with locked-in syndrome. Schools can be too readily locked into historic ways of doing, as inside a diving bell; if only they could take flight like the butterfly.

Along the way towards 2064, educators will go on debating and wrestling with, *inter alia*, such important questions as:

- What is the purpose of education: utilitarian, cultural transmission, career-orientated, person-orientated?

- What are the relevant roles of pre-primary, primary, secondary, further, higher education: do we have the right balance of resourcing for the different phases?

- What is the role of the school in the community? What is the relative importance of the school compared with that of the family and its social expectations?

- What makes a 'good school'? What are the requirements of a modern teacher? How do we best inspire, lead, educate, support the teaching profession? How do we attract teachers of the highest calibre?

- What is the role of inspection and consultancy in improving the school system?

- What matters more between the need for central standardisation and the desirability of local diversity?

- What is the meaning of talent, and how can individual needs/talents best be met? How much choice should pupils be allowed? How much freedom should they have to engage in driving their own learning, as opposed to 'taking in' given knowledge?

- How do we build a sense of self-worth and self-confidence in *all* children in an educational system built on competitive comparisons and performance grading?

The Greek philosophers taught the importance of constant disquisition. As the impatient optimist, at times in thrall to dangerous ideas, I see current and future generations of teachers ready to quest for brighter and better schools and classrooms, wherever I am in the world. They may even find solutions to some of the perennial questions above which exercise us today.

'I have seen the future, and it's very much like the present, only longer.'

Woody Allen

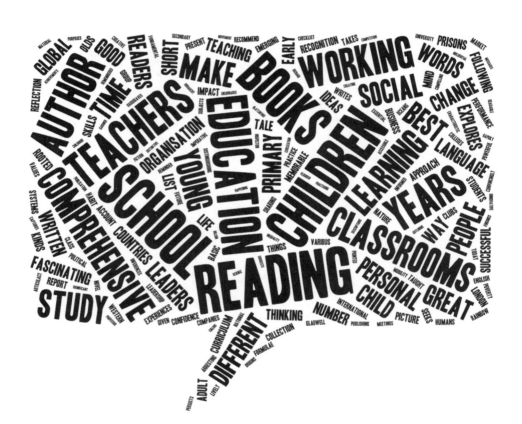

Chapter 14
A reading tale

He told us that the most dangerous parts of a book were invariably the bits to which you wanted to 'turn back to when alone'.

Joe O'Connor

Part A

Reading is fun and fundamental

Fresh out of university in 1973 and following a short stint working in a publishing house – I could not stand sitting behind a desk all day, so truanted – I began teaching adult literacy in HM Prison Brixton. Winston Churchill contested that one can judge a society by the way it treats its prisoners. All teachers should spend time in the education department of one of Her Majesty's prisons. It is a poignant reminder that basic literacy and articulacy are a birthright that should be denied no-one.

Between headships in the 1990s I had the fortune to work at the National Literacy Trust, leading the programme *Reading Is Fundamental UK*. Across the kingdom seven days of the week, we took books and writers to prisons, football clubs, women's refuges, miners' meeting rooms, kids-clubs, parks, shopping malls and diverse early years' settings – all with the intention of promoting the reading habit and love of books with families who didn't naturally buy or borrow books. On one occasion, indelibly sketched in my mind, we were revisiting a kids-club in Birmingham. A six year-old boy, whom I had met previously, asked me straight: 'Are you that man from reading is fun and mental?' Out of the mouths of babes...

At that time of the National Year of Reading I gave numerous presentations to emerging literacy collaboratives from Glasgow to Truro entitled 'Have you ever met a mugger who's read *Middlemarch*?' – my way of saying that whatever else we do for children and young people, we should give them the dignity of being able to speak, read and write with fluency in order to make their way in the endlessly fascinating global society which they inhabit.

Thus in schools, that imperative to get children reading happily and confidently is for me non-negotiable. In tandem must go creative, fun and persistent efforts by teachers to promote children's articulacy and fluent writing skills through recitation and performance of all kinds. As we all know, young children are sponges, and where language is modelled well with them, they will absorb and embed so much. It is of course the case that where children have impoverished language experiences in the home, schools must redouble their efforts to make a real difference.

The great linguist Noam Chomsky taught us convincingly about the basic language acquisition device possessed by all humans. Cognitive scientist Stephen Pinker has pointedly observed: 'A group of children is no more likely to invent an alphabet than it is to invent the internal combustion engine. Children are wired for sound, but print is an optional accessory that must be painstakingly bolted on.'

For all the well-meaning rhetoric which I hear in many western countries about social mobility, building a young person's self-confidence and personal social capital is deeply rooted in their facility with language in its many contemporary forms. We must get this right. Schools must ensure no child grows up with faltering language skills. *A child's reading age matching their chronological age* – for me, a manifesto for every school.

A reading approach

Chapter 7 includes a number of references to best classroom practice in literacy and oracy. What follows is a ready checklist which has informed my own teaching of reading down the years in a number of primary and secondary classrooms.

Reading across the curriculum

1. *Word recognition*

    - Division of words into syllables for pronunciation
    - Use of phonetic approach
    - Knowledge of prefixes and suffixes
    - Recognition of 'overtones' of words

2. *Vocabulary development*

    - Learning new words though wide reading
    - Learning keywords and concepts in various subjects
    - Learning technical abbreviations, symbols and formulae
    - Consulting dictionaries and thesaurus
    - Studying of words in various contexts
    - Study of word origins (etymology)
    - Recognition of common words

3. *Comprehension and organisation*

    - Comprehension of sentences accurately

- Comprehension of main idea of a paragraph
- Recognition of the organisation of an article or chapter
- Summarising what has been read
- Learning to read critically: distinguishing essential from non-essential, fact from opinion, noting cause and effect
- Drawing inferences and conclusions
- Reading 'between the lines'

4. *Reading interests*
   - Voluntary reading
   - Use of school and public library
   - Finding a personal value in reading
   - Appraisal of quality of reading material
   - Development of particular reading interests
   - Reading for personal information

5. *Study skills*
   - Sitting still long enough to read
   - Using skimming for different purposes
   - Reading maps, charts, graphs, diagrams, formulae
   - Learning how to take notes
   - Reading more rapidly with adequate comprehension
   - Forming the study habit.

In recent years I have taught reading to seven year-olds using the enchanting and beguiling picture-books of Anthony Browne, to develop a first understanding of inference. I have taught 11 year-olds to appreciate the compelling narratives of Harper Lee. I have coached 16 year-olds in GCSE non-fiction comprehension exercises. Different kinds of intervention work with different audiences. And the nature of teaching is that we may not get it right first time with a child who is having difficulties with basic decoding or not grasping metaphor.

Reflecting on the checklist above, skilled teachers will not make the mistake of adopting simply an age-related approach to the teaching of reading. Rather, they select what works for a given child or group of children at a particular point in time. They are driven by the unshakeable belief that every child in a mainstream school will leave their hands able to tackle texts with confidence, whether on the printed page or the Kindle.

Part B

Recommended reading

This reading list is divided into six sections, reflecting my own professional reading journeys. When working with busy teachers and school leaders I tend to recommend books which are short, accessible to the reader, and ones which have had an impact on or challenged my own thinking and practice. Another author will present another kind of list. In turn, the reader makes his or her own personal list, acting on recommendations.

When I was studying at the London Institute of Education in the early 1980s, Margaret Meek (editor of *The Cool Web*) memorably reminded us that when we came to read in the course of our career *Of Mice and Men* for the fourteenth time with a GCSE class, and I did, the teacher should always remember that it would be the *first* time for the student. *Farmer Duck* and *Rainbow Fish* (listed below) should be shared in the same spirit with every new generation of young readers.

Some people deliberately choose to read a daily newspaper that challenges their own views, while others read a paper that reinforces their values, prejudices and mind-set. These listings should promote response and stimulate ideas, in whatever direction.

1. Schools and schooling

An Education Service for the Whole Community, ILEA, 1973

A pioneering report produced under the leadership of Peter Newsam, Education Officer for the Inner London Education Authority. It set out a vision for early years, schools, youth and adult education which has shaped community education to this day.

The Comprehensive School, I.G.K. Fenwick, 1976

Written during the first wave of 'comprehensivisation', this is both an historical core text for students of the English school system, and a reflection of the then political optimism for comprehensive education being able to promote social mobility.

The Challenge for the Comprehensive School, David Hargreaves, 1982

By the early 1980s, cracks in the comprehensive ideal were emerging, particularly in London where the author became Chief Inspector. Hargreaves captures these cracks trenchantly, and in characteristic style seeks to address emerging problems with innovative, creative new ways of doing.

The Harpole Report, J.L. Carr, 2003

One of the best short, amusing reads on the life of a primary school, merging fact and fiction. A beleaguered headmaster tells his tale.

Politics Markets & America's Schools, Chubb & Moe, 1990

A seminal book in thinking about schooling across western democracies. Written on the back of 1980s urban breakdown in the US, the authors launched a debate about whether schooling should be taken from the hands of politicians and given over to the market.

Handsworth Revolution, David Winkley, 2002

One headteacher's personal, humorous and superbly crafted account of transforming a large Birmingham primary school, set against the backcloth of demographic, social and political change through the last two decades of the twentieth century.

The Diving-Bell and the Butterfly, Jean-Dominique Bauby, 1997

The very moving account of a chief executive of a publishing company who is struck down with locked-in syndrome. Actually put onto page by an amanuensis following the author's eye-blinks, the narrative has all kinds of resonances for leaders, their strictures and their freedoms.

School Wars, Melissa Benn, 2011

One of the most readable accounts of what is happening in English education today, with the advent of the academy and free school movement. Raising fascinating echoes of 'The Challenge for the Comprehensive School' (above), the author reasserts the values of local community comprehensive education, and outlines the social perils of losing that imperative.

The Tail, Paul Marshall, 2013

A collection of essays which pulls no punches in saying to teachers and leaders everywhere that expectations of what children and young people *can* achieve must be raised. Rooted in the academy movement in London of the past few years, the various contributors present their ideas on school transformation, benchmarked against the world's best.

2. 21st century aspirations

Good to Great and the Social Sectors, Jim Collins, 2001

Based on the author's original tome on how large companies move from good to great, this slim volume applies Collins's first principles to how schools, churches, hospitals and charities might move from good to great: 'A great organisation is one that delivers superior performance and makes a distinctive impact over a long period of time.'

How the world's best-performing school systems come out on top, McKinsey, 2007

This report explores the system ingredients of those countries and jurisdictions with successful schools, when comparing their students' achievements. Its focus on recruiting the brightest and best into teaching and investing in their training has had a significant impact on global school systems. A later report from the same source is titled 'How the world's most improved school systems keep getting better'.

The Spirit Level, Wilkinson/Pickett, 2009

An arresting read about equality and inequalities in different countries, and how education provision and outcomes are at the core. For readers who enjoy their statistical bar-charts and graphs, this book is fascinating to ponder over and hypothesise on possible solutions to reducing social inequality.

The Bottom Billion, Paul Collier, 2007

Global poverty is falling rapidly but still a billion of the world's people live in abject poverty. This is an arresting analysis of why certain countries appear resolutely entrapped in their poverty pit – worth sharing with teachers and students of any subject discipline.

The Tipping Point, Malcolm Gladwell, 2000

The author explores how little things can make a difference in any organisation or business, and what it takes to effect just small changes which can lead to significant organisational shift, development and success. USA-rooted, but applicable globally.

Blink, Malcolm Gladwell, 2005

Subtitled 'the power of thinking without thinking', this powerful collection of essays explores how experts in their particular fields can cut to the chase of what works. In the context of education, Gladwell asks: how long did it take you to decide how good your professor at college was? And could you trust that first judgement?

Nudge, Thaler & Sunstein, 2008

This is a compelling study of what it takes to change social behaviours in many everyday contexts. Do humans respond best to being told what to do, or nudged towards changing their habits? The narrative has proved influential reading amongst global policy makers in recent years.

Oceans of Innovation, Barber, Donnelly, Rizvi, 2012

A short, highly readable account of what is happening globally in education systems, where they have come from, and what each is seeking to 'steal' from others in creating world-class education. There are no magic formulae suggested, but rather common approaches tailored to specific contexts.

The Triple Package, Rubenfield and Chua, 2014

In a world where living and working outside the country of your birth has become the norm for millions of people, this is a fascinating and provocative exploration of what cultural traits and other factors drive immigrants and different groups of people to be successful.

3. Leadership

Do nothing to change your life, Stephen Cottrell, 2007

Written when he was Bishop of Reading (now Bishop of Chelmsford) the author encourages us to 'nurture our inner slob'. There are some simple and important messages about humans *being* as well as doing.

The Three Ways of Getting Things Done, Gerard Fairtlough, 2005

Short, unorthodox study of how to challenge hierarchies in organisations. Through anecdote and example, this former CEO of Shell Chemicals UK writes convincingly about how and why hierarchy is not the only way to run a successful business, school or hospital.

Blue Ocean Strategy, Chan Kim & Renee Mauborgne, 2005

Rooted in studies of international companies and containing a fair amount of business-speak, the authors' ideas around creating 'uncontested market space' and breaking out of 'the red ocean of bloody competition' have something distinctive to offer leaders in schools and colleges.

Why should anyone be led by you?, Goffer & Jones, 2006

These authors are remembered for introducing into the leadership lexicon the phrase 'authentic chameleons', a fair description in many contexts. As the title suggests, they also hold the mirror up to leaders through a number of intriguing case studies.

Lessons from the Top, Gavin Esler, 2012

From American Presidents to rock stars and criminals, the broadcaster Gavin Esler is fascinated by the stories leaders tell, for good and ill, in order to persuade their followers and voters. Plenty of rich material for school assemblies here.

4. Curriculum

Unweaving The Rainbow, Richard Dawkins, 1998

Distinguished professor of science and self-professed atheist, Dawkins has written a number of memorable books. Here he seeks to explore and explain the beauty of nature, refuting any myth and superstition. 'The Magic of Reality' (2012) is a companion volume for children, handsomely illustrated.

Five Minds for the Future, Howard Gardner, 2008

Many teachers know Gardner's work on multiple intelligences. This equally accessible book spells out what the lively twenty-first century mind might look like, whether a child's or an adult's.

Civilization, Niall Ferguson, 2011

A must-read for any educated teacher: what is it about civilization in Western Europe that has allowed it to flourish, often at the expense of other empires? And will the 21st century see that change? Democracy, science, consumerism, the work ethic, competition, medicine – each 'killer app' is brilliantly analysed.

Future Files: A brief history of the next 50 years, Richard Watson, 2010

Watson is among the most thought-provoking and convincing of current futurologists, imagining alternative futures and helping readers see 'familiar things in a new light and unfamiliar things with greater clarity'.

Taking Forward the Primary Curriculum, Roy Blatchford, 2013

A collection of essays from practising teachers and school leaders outlining their ideas on what makes for a great primary curriculum, today and for tomorrow.

Education and Learning, Mellanby & Theobald, 2014

Based on many years of research – in classrooms and university laboratories – the book aims to bring its extensive findings about how and why and where children best learn to the attention of classroom practitioners.

5. Classrooms

The Schoolmaster, A.C. Benson, 1902

Few practising teachers have surpassed this teacher's clear and pithy descriptions of the craft of the classroom. Written in the early 20th century - just as relevant today.

The Other Side of the Dale, Gervase Phinn, 1998

The first of many collections of stories by this author about life on the road as a school inspector. Wit, passion, compassion and love of children and classrooms shine though every page. Excellent for assemblies and staff meetings.

The Learning Game, Jonathan Smith, 2000

One teacher's tale of classroom encounters, and of both his personal and professional experiences of fellow teachers, staffrooms and the real ups-and-downs of any career. Some real reflection and wisdom.

Teacher Man, Frank McCourt, 2005

Best known for his novel 'Angela's Ashes', the author brings to life here his experiences as a teacher – handsomely written.

Sparkling Classrooms, Roy Blatchford, 2011

The author has visited 10,000 lessons in schools and colleges around the world. In this short monograph, he seeks to capture the essence of memorable classrooms.

Bounce: how champions are made, Matthew Syed, 2010

A book which has been influential in current thinking about how children and young people come to make good progress in their schooling and out-of-school activities. Is it through purposeful practice, innate abilities, the encouragement of teachers and parents, feedback, opportunities given and taken – what's the cocktail?

6. Childhood

As If, Blake Morrison, 1997

The author takes the case of a notorious murder of a child by two other children to explore the importance of childhood, and those pressures which threaten to crowd it out. There have been a number of similar books since its first publication, but few as well observed as this one.

The Boy in the Striped Pyjamas, John Boyne, 2006

An arresting read, for children and adult alike, but a novel which is now widely studied in primary and secondary schools. Comparisons are often drawn between the text and the film based on the book.

Farmer Duck, Waddell & Oxenbury, 1991

One of the great picture-books in the English language, with its echoes of Orwell's 'Animal Farm', and an unfailing success with young readers.

Rainbow Fish, Marcus Pfister, 1992

An international bestseller: this tale of sharing, enchantingly drawn, is one of the most ubiquitous picture-books in primary classrooms.

Once upon an ordinary school day, McNaughton & Kitamura, 2005

Another enchanting picture-book, with a message for teachers as powerful as the narrative which unfolds for young children.

Proust and the Squid, Maryanne Wolf, 2008

This is a learned examination – with many memorable examples – of the reading brain, its workings and malfunctions. For the reader who persists, it is full of game-changing observations.

The woman who walked into doors, Roddy Doyle, 1996

The author is known for his raw, rude and witty observations of working-class life on Dublin estates. In this novel, the focus is on an abusive relationship within a marriage and how that impacts upon the children. Characteristic of Roddy Doyle, children survive and even flourish.

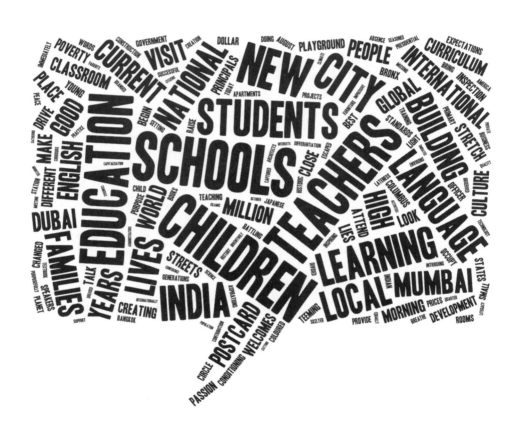

Chapter 15

International postcards

Wake up in the morning
Stretch your arms towards the sun
Say something in Chinese
And go to Paris....
Every minute, somewhere in the world there is morning
Somewhere, people stretch their arms towards the sun
They speak new languages, fly from Cairo to Warsaw
They smile and drink coffee together.

Anastasia Baburova

POST CARD **from New York, June 2007**

For readers not familiar with the New York subway system, both Columbus Circle and Elder Avenue are stations on the same line.

Columbus Circle lies at the fashionable end of Eighth Avenue. The spectacular, half-submerged glass cube that is the Apple Computer shop does roaring business close by. A restaurant tab for four at the local Mandarin Oriental will set you back $500. A penthouse flat overlooking Central Park close by the station changed hands this week for $50 million. The people here are seriously rich, look and feel it, shaded by Japanese maples and parasols. Even Scott Fitgerald would turn his head at the wealth of the current era.

Take the 6 Train a dozen subway stops north and you arrive at Elder Avenue, in the heart of the Bronx.

Stepping out of the station, the dirt and shimmering heat of the streets are immediate. Diners run by Puerto Ricans sell breakfast for a dollar. The housing projects are where people live: in the land of acronyms and brash capitalisation, NYPD Operation Clean Halls is the sign that welcomes. All global life is here, teeming onto the streets by way of escape from the cramped apartments and humming air-conditioning. A cruising Buick, boot open to reveal four-foot high speakers, thumps out its dramatic and deafening bass. Different generations, poverty a shared experience, barbecue food on the doorsteps.

This is America's most successful big city, a city divided.

Arriving at one of New York's many new schools in the Bronx, I show my ID to the resident police officers. I soon realise that this is not one school, but three occupying the same building. Part of Mayor Bloomberg's drive to raise standards (only 50% of the city's high school students graduate in four years) has been to create small schools with an extraordinary array of aspirational names. Choice is the talisman. Many high schools now number around 300 students in an attempt to create units where children feel safe and free from the gang culture that still grips their lives on the streets.

I ask innocently of a group of 15 year-olds why, if life can be so grim in the housing projects and school is a place of welcome and safety, attendance is so low. 'Some just don't make it here', comes the wistful reply. One student talks of his friend having 'taken a dollar and fifty bucks', a reference to a slashed face of 150 stitches.

Visiting a number of elementary, middle and high schools on the wrong side of the tracks, certain themes emerge. A number of the principals I encounter have lived the lives of the children they serve. One grew up in the failing local high school, escaped to an Ivy League college and has returned to her neighbourhood to raise expectations and ambitions. Another attended the same building her new school now occupies. Many teachers went to local schools and have a passionate commitment to serving and inspiring local children. Presidential candidate Barack Obama's biography *The Audacity of Hope* is on the bestsellers lists here, the title a neat summary of what many of these educators breathe.

One small school has had three principals in the three years since its creation – and two different buildings. Children travel from miles around: lateness is chronic and absence endemic. The current inspirational principal is about restoring order to fractured lives, striving against all odds to drive forward developments in classroom practice. One lean and fit boy in the school observed he was 'puttin' on a fat belly' because at lunchtime everyone stays inside the canteen, a necessity with no playground.

Another theme is the learning environment. Architects shape golden lives at Columbus Circle and environs, while school buildings in many parts of the Bronx, Brooklyn and Queens are in need of significant refurbishment. Décor is drab, classroom furniture is tired, and hallways and stairwells are bleak. By sharp contrast, in the new purpose-built schools, one an imaginatively converted factory, rooms are light, air-conditioned and fit for purpose.

Which leads me to the curriculum. Blackboards are being installed in new schools, while smartboards are conspicuous by their absence. Information technology as we know it in UK schools is in its infancy here in the domain of Disney and Google. English language arts, math, social studies and a smattering of textbook science provide the diet of most children and students.

Music, gym and global history depend on facilities and teacher recruitment. Design & Technology, geography and MFL are nowhere to be seen. Any talk of a uniform national curriculum and national tests is politically unacceptable, with the Federal government contributing just nine cents out of each dollar spent on schools.

Yet in the wake of the indelibly branded No Child Left Behind law, US schools are gripped by their students making AYP: adequate yearly progress in reading and math tests. Teaching is not mentioned, rather it is all about instructional programs. Chalk and talk is a common mode of delivery. Differentiation and data are the new buzz words, but I reassure my hosts that pendulums swing, from Plowden to Woodhead and back again.

Just where the children of families who occupy the Columbus Circle apartments attend school I've not yet visited. That's for another postcard. There was a time in US politics when poverty was a critical component of presidential campaigns. With 2008 election-specials beginning to dominate the myriad TV channels, the poor and their educational aspirations appear to be kept out of sight in this city of plenty.

***

POST CARD
from Mumbai, August 2008

What once was Bombay is now Mumbai. Poona has become Pune, Madras is now Chennai. There's chatter of India being recast as Hindustan. For his readers E.M. Forster characterised the country as a place of confusions and paradox. Vikram Seth captured its colour, aromas and family intrigues, Ruth Prawer Jhabvala its heat and its dust. Yet no fictional account can begin to evoke the fascinating variety and teeming action that is India.

To survive on India's roads the adage runs: good horn, good brakes, good driver and very good luck. During Mumbai's monsoon season signs urge 'Drive carefully – someone is waiting for you'. And the truth is that everyone does hurtle along with extraordinary care, horns blaring excessively yet somehow purposefully.

No rush-hour in New York, London or Sydney can match the frantic, steaming chaos that Mumbai displays. Unimaginable loads are being pulled, pushed and carried by men, women and children. Auto-ricks, yoked oxen, horses, battered buses, packed baby-taxis and improbably laden cars miss each other miraculously in this restless city of 20 million souls.

In Juhu, Marine Drive and Malabar Hill lies some of the most expensive and glitzy real-estate on the planet. The price of lunch at the Oberoi Hotel is a month's wages for those who serve it. The Raj and its gentlemen's clubs linger in places. HSBC, Kodak and Nokia jostle with Tata and Mittal for brand supremacy. This is an amazing urban spread, divided by caste.

'Slum Dwellers International' proclaims a hoarding on a new building site sweeping away a tented village. Walk along the pavements around Crawford Market and whole families live beneath blue tarpaulin strung out between trees, their bathroom the drains, their cooker an open fire, their belongings scant – and all under the relentless, August monsoon rain.

The closer you look, the more people you glimpse: resilient and peaceful millions eke out an existence in a city that is changing at a helter-skelter pace. And from shacks and shanty towns all over Mumbai, early each morning millions of children appear impeccably dressed for school, their clothes washed and 'pressed' each evening. They are India's wonderfully bright and optimistic future, valuing an education that they and their parents know will deliver them from their current grinding poverty.

It's not just the children who are starry-eyed about their futures. Teachers I've been working with are equally intent on revolutionising the state of India's education system. Increasing numbers of young teachers are challenging the status quo, setting up their own low fee-paying schools to bring literacy to the 'untouchables'.

Currently, individual class sizes can hit over 80, with 50+ the average in many government schools. In this context, differentiation can mean little: rote learning is a prevailing and effective survival tool for teachers. Chalk and talk permeate. Books are dated, well-worn but scrupulously cared for. Homework satchels abound, and rarely do homework diaries go missing.

One classroom I enter is in fact a former chapel, housing over 90 twelve year-olds, with two teachers battling each other's voices in the gloom. The three-language framework means Hindi and Maharastran are the languages of the playground and the corridors. English is the medium of learning. Boys and girls alike write with a consistent accuracy and fluency that would shame a quarter of primary children in the UK.

On Independence Day (August 15), schools are closed for normal business; children assemble in lines, perform their drills, and the flag is raised. Gandhi's legacy is everywhere, not least in the national curriculum's celebration of peace as an integral way of Indians being and doing. Our own flirtations with peace studies are put firmly in the shade.

I visit one school which houses weekly boarders, boys from the poorest of families. At 8.30am – unsupervised – they have packed away their floor-bedding into lockers, washed and dressed, and commenced private study. Their great good humour and quiet determination to succeed and support one another strike any visitor.

Beyond Mumbai to the east lies the city of Pune and its surrounding green and lush hills. Property prices are booming. In the countryside seven-room primary schools are being built by local social entrepreneurs wishing to transform the life chances of tribal and nomadic children. There are few books, bare walls, basic furniture and poor sanitation. But there are dedicated trainee teachers and support staff with a will to bring literacy, numeracy and the arts to eager young minds.

There is a ubiquitous pride in and valuing of education which the West is slowly losing, has lost some would argue. To visit just a small corner of India today is to witness a great nation on the march. Whether it can modernise without westernising, the next few decades will tell.

What many, many educators are doing today with India's children is at once captivating and humbling.

***

POST CARD   from Dubai, April 2009

The Dubai skyline exceeds expectations, refracting desert sun with a shattering intensity. Buildings like sculptured pokers defy the expected rules of gravity. Reputedly, a quarter of the world's construction cranes are hosted here, many in suspended animation courtesy of the global slow-down. Echoes of Ozymandias and his 'vast and trunkless legs of stone' resonate.

White, white sand and vivid green lawns lie side by side as though splashed from a child's paint-box. Desalinated water is the liquid gold. The apocryphal shopping malls beat to a consumer drum almost alone now on the planet. A breathtaking helter-skelter bisects one mall, another sports the largest snow-dome ever constructed. Atlantis is the famed water-park guaranteed to thrill children and terrify parents in equal measure.

The sheer scale takes your breath away. A billboard stretching out across the sands heralds 'Another 19 million square feet of quality healthcare'. The *next* international airport under construction has a footprint the size of Swindon, while the grand design of the current one dwarfs quaint Terminal 5 at Heathrow.

Overstated opulence and understated poverty lie uncomfortably close together. The army of ants who crawl over every building site are largely Indian workers earning $200 a month. The same sum buys tea for two in the iconic Burj Al Arab, the landmark hotel floating on its own man-made island.

This is a city where prospectors have arrived like a gold rush, a modern-day Tower of Babel. Yet dig behind the surface glitz and there is a renewed vision of a society which stretches back to antiquity.

'Education. Education. Education.' Familiar words? They are the clarion call of Sheikh Mohammed Al-Maktoum, ruler of Dubai. The Knowledge and Human Development Agency was born a few years ago with the express aim of creating a knowledge and skills economy to rival the best. Intent on ensuring a world-class schools system, the Dubai Schools Inspection Bureau is auditing every establishment, public and private, in its jurisdiction. All curriculum models are here: UAE, Indian, IB, German, Iranian, US, Russian, Philippine, Japanese.

Amidst a fascinating educational diaspora, my interest is captured by the government provision.

Journeys to visit schools begin in impossible rush-hour traffic, continue on spacious highways of ingenious engineering, and end down dusty tracks best negotiated by 4x4s and a driver with a good horn. Welcomes to the playground begin with a hundred handshakes, followed in the Principal's office by black Arabic coffee and a platter of delicious sweetmeats – and it's only 7am.

Inspecting and reviewing schools through an interpreter arrests one's seasoned eyes and ears. Leadership and management, teaching and learning, students' personal development – the key ingredients don't change essentially from Dubai to Mumbai, New York to London. Yet cultural nuances matter profoundly.

In one school I watch a skilled team of teachers of English make me look afresh at my own language. Native speakers of Arabic, with few resources beyond a lacklustre textbook and battling the incessant air-conditioning, impress with their passion for the subject – a desire to open up new horizons for the children they serve. During a later meeting they are thirsty for professional development. We discuss how English as a language is being reconfigured, fabulously and inventively, by billions of people around the world who are making it their Esperanto.

In a desert climate, children react to rare torrential rain in the way UK children respond to a few inches of snow: a mad dash for the playground to soak themselves. Attendance is down in one school, according to the welfare officer, 'because it rained yesterday'. We know it rained because whole hallways and corridors are drying out.

At another school, Tuesday morning sees suspension of the normal timetable in pursuit of mixed-age learning activities, chosen by the children. Some are dual storytelling in Arabic and English; some are running a fresh fruit stall; others are cutting up fresh fish, while others still are creating brightly coloured artefacts linked to their Islamic Studies.

Assemblies are unashamedly nationalistic and rooted in Islam. They are led powerfully by the children and, in this climate, are held outdoors to everyone's pleasure. They cause me to reflect on the purpose of the many hundreds of assemblies I have led and observed: what does it mean to be a British citizen today, and do we celebrate this?

All Grade 8 students, boys and girls alike, have a module of active civic duty, school and community based with smart uniforms provided. These young 21st century citizens have an impressive understanding of their allegiances to both Dubai and the United Arab Emirates, and of its historic creation in 1971 out of the Trucial States.

Here lies a different axis of power. The Emirates look west historically to Europe and America, but their current and future interests lie profoundly with one another, and with India and China.

An interesting debate unfolds in the pages of the *Gulf News*: should there be a quota for expatriate students in public schools that would allow children from different cultures to meet? And this in a city where only about 15% of the total population are Emiratis, the rest from just about any place you can name on the planet.

What particular images am I left with? Primary-aged children marching with rifles as part of the curriculum; short plays enacting the Middle East conflict which challenge my own prejudices; feeding back inspection findings to a team of women robed in burkas; joyful children hungry for learning and a passion to learn English; teachers, creative as they are the world over.

***

POST CARD — from Bangkok, October 2012

What is it that brings nearly one in ten of Thailand's teachers to Bangkok for three days during their October mid-term break?

For those brought up in the UK on geography and history books from the 1960s, this is the Kingdom of Siam, its temples, buddhas and historic battles with neighbouring Burma. Contemporary tourist guides on this south-east Asian hub city describe it as 'beguiling and bewildering, subtle and brash, spiritual and sensual'.

On the Bangkok streets, there is the buzz of a teeming, multi-cultural, multi-lingual city with a young population, content in its own skin and underpinned by the quiet certainties of its religions. As in India, the older generation is revered and family ties are strong, evident at dusk as families dine modestly together in their doorways and shop entrances.

What have the 40,000 teachers come to? It's EDUCA 2012, an annual gathering where teachers can catch up on what local, national and international educators are thinking, doing and designing. There is a hunger for high quality in-service that is humbling, and not an ounce of cynicism. Pride of place is a group photo in front of the enormous conference programme board.

The Minister of State for Education, with considerable entourage, takes the stage in the Grand Ballroom to the sounds of heavy-bass rock, and warmly welcomes the 2000 delegates gathered for the opening presentations. Smart 20-somethings skip around with cameras and microphones. The Minister responsible for IT in schools speaks with passion about the programme to provide every child with a tablet for learning. There is real ambition here to compete with the best education globally.

A myriad of workshops run from eight-til-late, held in a maze of superbly furnished rooms, outstripping in comfort, temperature and light most major UK conference centres (take note Olympia!). It's the sheer size of the workshop audiences that bedazzle: two or three hundred hanging on the speaker's every word and slide. I take in a fascinating presentation on the design of rural and urban schools, Thai architects harnessing light in intriguing ways for maximum benefit to teachers and students.

Global publisher Pearson is promoting classrooms of the future alongside inventive materials for language, maths and science teaching. And just beside them, local companies are demonstrating visualizers, smartboards and portable devices.

What gradually dawns on me as I wander further into the cavernous exhibition spaces is that these Thai teachers can buy just about anything here, from ties and knickers to umbrellas and suits, and at bargain prices. There is a jolly amount of sparkling tat too, fondly bagged up for family members back home.

On the international platform we hear about transformations in China's teacher training and its unfathomable numbers of new teachers; about 'education miracle' Finland which has had to ration visits from overseas educators in search of Finnish ways to PISA success; about 'teacher-preneurs' in the US, a cadre of innovative teachers seeking to spread best classroom practice beyond their own schools and states.

My own contribution shares the new DfE Teachers' Standards and the merits of a national inspection system, the latter not immediately attractive to the Thai culture, though administrators are open to its potential as the nation seeks to benchmark its standards internationally.

Two final images. Fifty early years' teachers purposefully cutting out and colouring to music, so focused they didn't blink at our cameras. Then 1800 teachers singing together as they problem solved in mathematics, led by an engaging duo harnessing visualizer and YouTube to magical effect. You couldn't make it up.

Chapter 16

From the archives

Ah, but I was so much older then
I'm younger than that now.

My Back Pages, Bob Dylan

CENTRAL RESERVATIONS

Times Educational Supplement   *May 1990*

If wholesale privatization of the welfare state is to be headed off, the public sector as we know it needs to be rejuvenated and effectively marketed. Above all, the vocabulary of "private" versus "public" needs burying.

What does this mean for education? Down the local management road a year or two, with our computer networks up and running, what will be the role of local education authorities? Indeed, if we take the "pure" model of grant-maintained schools what are an authority's obligations now: home-school transport; ensuring parents comply with the law on school attendance; special-needs assessment; certain board-and-lodging charges, bursaries and providing clothing for pupils? What else is the authority of the future to offer schools and colleges?

On this page last September, Margaret Maden, former headteacher and now Warwickshire county education officer, argued that the successful authority of the 1990s will be "characterized by its operational efficiency, its responsiveness and by its networking function," a description which caused one letter-writer to quip: "Her vision of some new ultra-lubricated, high-performing bureaucratic machine is my nightmare."

Margaret Maden warned of the dangers of foisting "the managerial model of big business on to the education service". She is right: LMS is not about keeping shareholders happy with year-end profits. But it *is* about long-term planning and reinvestment. It is crucially about deciding which aspects of schools should be run with public sector solutions and which with those of the market place.

Her view of the importance of the education authority's systematical approach to training and its role in monitoring and evaluation should not be under-estimated. But can it be claimed that the needs of schools are best served by the permanent terms of officers and advisers that have been an unchanged and hitherto unquestioned part of authority provision? Consultancies surely beckon.

Perhaps the most hollow of her "New networks for old" was the assertion that "the intricate connections between legal, personnel and curricular issues represent a valuable resource". Again, can we say that the interaction between subject inspectors, personnel officers and property planning departments has provided the coherent service schools and colleges will now be expecting?

Local education authorities are all busy re-organizing but in *different* ways, a certain sign that their future is hazy.

Responsiveness and accountability lie at the heart of the effective community school; the school which is public not private with its aims and achievements. The public sector can be distant and inefficient; but these are not features of being public *per se*.

I have believed – optimistically – since the early drafts of the Education Reform Act that where LMS will succeed splendidly is in highlighting for parents and governors the underfunding of state education. The same people will also come to see that the existence of local authorities in their present form perpetuates, within a national service, marked and indefensible discrepancies in the cost of a child's education from one part of the country to another. And how long will it be before governing bodies question the notion that 11-year-olds are "worth" more in the financial formulas than nine-year-olds?

Unless urgent change is forthcoming education authorities may come to be viewed as outmoded units within the democratic process and as repositories of bloated bureaucracy and over-regulation. They once served to equalize resources across an area and were a pivotal fount of social justice. We need to relocate that pivot in the wake of formula funding, and in ways which hold true to the values of comprehensive education and dampen the worst excesses of competition and market-led schooling.

One way forward surely lies in education into the 21st century being run by district boards or neighbourhood partnerships. While I would not subscribe to the poisoned chalice of "opting out" I would opt in to locally-managed partnerships of primary and secondary schools, and the evolution of all-through institutions for the delivery of 0-90 continuing education – or "sperm to worm" as one colleague insists on terming it.

My vision of district partnerships in towns, villages and cities has as its base a locally-determined continuity charter for children and parents: continuity in learning progression and family involvement in a child's education. Each partnership would be tied in closely with a teacher-training institution for professional development and to counter parochialism.

The management of physical-plant, of domestic services, of special needs, of monitoring and evaluation, and much more would take place at that local level, with links into social services, youth and adult provision, and libraries, all carrying a vital sense of neighbourhood.

There is much here to be learned from the American district boards in relation to the real involvement of parents and teachers in the governance of schools and colleges.

The singular problem of our service for the past 20 years has been our collective failure to market state education. Headteachers and governors need to seize that initiative, and nowhere better than with locally-based educationalists alongside employers, developers and councillors who have an interest in their own backyards. We need to embrace a form of federalism in which the initiative, drive and energy come from the schools and colleges.

Should education authorities be rehearsing their exit lines? As presently structured, I believe so. Their mission statement and strategic planning must redefine the role of the system's centre. The limpets should not prevail.

If we are to hold on to the values of comprehensive education through to the next century – irrespective of central government persuasion and community charge contribution to education funding – authority managers, governing bodies, teachers and headteachers should, together, now begin to shape a system that moves towards true local responsiveness in the interest of high-quality learning for young people.

***

IN LEAGUE, NOT IN TABLES

Times Educational Supplement   *May 1992*

Two years ago I wrote in the *TES* that, irrespective of central government persuasion, the future of state-funded education lay in neighbourhood partnerships for education from 3 to 19, each with its own locally determined "continuity charter for children and parents: continuity in learning progression and family involvement in a child's education". As teachers and governors begin to rehearse their exit lines from local authority control, the values of partnership need to be marketed if we are to preserve a single-tier system for the nation's children.

The advent of fully delegated budgets has led many neighbouring schools –primary and secondary; first, middle and upper; junior and senior high – to ask questions as to how they might work more collaboratively. If their starting point is to reverse the history of schools and governing bodies working separately –albeit within the LEA framework – then what might follow is a vision of the future management of education very much in partnership rather than in competition. As one group of headteachers recently proclaimed: "working in league but not in tables".

Schools clearly find themselves in different environments, with varying histories and agendas. In some parts of the country, a philosophy of collaboration may seem profoundly at odds with other powerful forces in the local community. Yet the hurdles of falling rolls, traditionally determined catchment areas and selective schools can be overcome if educators come together in the interest of enhancing the quality of their 3 to 19 provision.

Even the first tentative steps towards closer links between a cluster of adjacent schools raises searching questions about teachers' practice, governing bodies' autonomy, parental attitudes, resources and their location, and eventually implications for the appointment of teaching and non-teaching staff.

The effective partnership will need to prepare itself to manage and respond to these issues. Challenging long-held assumptions about educating either five-year-olds or sixteen-year-olds rather than all youngsters in a 3 to 19 partnership is essential for this public service in the 1990s. A critical starting point for governors will be to examine the historic LEA age-weighting of pupils.

What can a flourishing partnership mean in practice? The national curriculum has given teachers and families a much-needed curriculum map. But much remains to be done to ensure continuity and progression. There are still too many folds in the map – usually at the point of transfer from one school to the next. Partnership will enable a planned gradient of learning through the years of compulsory schooling, with information about programmes of study, assessment and special needs published in a common format for all parents in a local community.

Secondary schools might be prompted to review successful family workshops and paired reading schemes beyond the primary years, while teachers of nine and ten-year-olds may look more assiduously at formal homework timetables. And as teachers across a partnership begin to share their subject specialisms, opportunities for extending the more able child are clearly seen.

There is little doubt that open enrolment is a growing source of disquiet to primary and secondary schools alike. A partnership holding unambiguously to certain ground rules can minimise the worst excesses of market-led education. A common contract with families can be published, making clear the basic rules and expectations and how families will be supported, where appropriate, by external agencies such as educational psychologists and social services. Too often some families will play one school against another, to everybody's loss.

The past year or two has seen some exciting developments between schools in the field of resource management, from sharing bursars and purchasing meals, to grounds maintenance and a register of supply teachers; from pooling IT, sports and music equipment to sharing reprographic costs and foreign language assistants. Co-operative ventures have been glimpsed by enterprising managers and look destined to break boundaries.

Yet it is in the area of professional development that schools stand most to gain through partnership arrangements. Teacher secondments within a cluster of schools to devise, for example, a technology transfer document or an art bridging topic; teachers using one another for self-evaluation and inspection; joint teacher appointments across the 9 to 13 range; links with higher education as training becomes properly more school-focused. Opportunities for primary and secondary teachers, together, to lead developments in learning and teaching are nothing short of exhilarating and will offer a much-needed sense of empowerment to the profession.

In relation to all of the above, the key questions are: what can an individual school do effectively? What can a partnership of schools do effectively? Eurospeak has brought us the word "subsidiarity". It is exactly that concept which schools contemplating self-management should reflect hard upon.

Central government has rightly thrown down the gauntlet to the public services of discovering ways to modernise without privatising. And marketing what we are doing has a crucial role to play in all this. Marketing does not have to mean naked competition which is intent on burying the opposition. Indeed, it is the first law of commercial enterprise that cartels follow hard on the heels of competition. One need look no further than the way major supermarkets responded to a break in the Sunday trading laws.

It is no longer sufficient for schools to talk of "serving the community": the community has to be defined and its needs established. The life-cycle of commercial marketing has to become the lifeblood of schools working together: market research, product development, promotion, quality control. Alongside this cycle schools need to examine thoughtfully the buzz themes of the Citizen's Charter – standards, quality, value and choice.

A partnership of schools working in tandem with its local community can set about a systematic audit of what it is offering and thereby enhance its service to families.

It is not possible to market a poor product for very long: what it says on the jar must be matched by the jar's contents.

Some LEAs have had the vision to anticipate trends of schools clustering together; Oxfordshire is one such that intends to redeploy its existing Primary Development Fund as a Partnership Development Fund. Perhaps that way local authorities can find a new role. Whatever the final outcome of "opt-out" discussions in the coming months, school staff and governing bodies need to cherish the values of working together, to market their product, and to go on improving value for money to their family customers.

***

REFORM OF THE ROUTE TO HIGHER EDUCATION IS NOW LONG OVERDUE

Education   *October 1993*

The August roller coaster of students' emotions, not to mention those of their families and teachers, upon receipt of GCSE and A level results is an annual reminder that the present systems are stuttering.

Take first the structure of the 14-19 curriculum and its schemes of assessment, well overdue for revision. Second, methods of entry to, and the very organization of, higher education are increasingly out of step with the National Education and Training Targets. Without reform, we are unlikely to see 50 per cent of young people reaching NVQ level 3, equivalent to 2+ A levels, by the year 2000.

It is Brutus who reminds us that:

There is a tide in the affairs of men,
Which, taken at the flood, leads on to fortune;
Omitted, all the voyage of their life
Is bound in shallows and in miseries.

Two overlapping reform tides command our present attention. Wise, collaborative initiative is needed from central Government and the educational establishment. This will require that the former shifts from its preoccupation with short-term solutions, while the latter must prove willing to accept that inertia should not prevail.

In common with most headteachers up and down the country I spent most of August fielding matters arising from GCSE and A results. First came the mid-month cries of anguish and delight from 18 year olds. As widely and honestly reported, this year's cohort divided neatly out into C P Snow's two cultures. Maths and science candidates have moved effortlessly into their first-choice universities, even those who slipped a point or two. In striking – and galling – contrast Arts students, even those with A and B grades, have struggled to secure their chosen place of study where the upper grades happen to have come out in the wrong order.

How do you explain to frantic parents that despite securing the overall UCCA points total required their son is now not able to go to the city to which he has been preparing to move since the university made its offer, eight months ago? How do you console a 'rejected' geography student who knows she has worked harder than her physics counterpart only to see the friend accepted with lower grades?

Happily, reform in at least one direction is imminent: the UCCA/PCAS divide is to be dissolved. For too long it has perpetuated parental and student prejudices about alleged first and second class institutions, a point not helped by clearing places lists in national newspapers insisting on the terms 'old' and 'new' universities. How long will it be before we see the birth of a British Ivy League?

A week later in August saw the arrival of GCSE results, with attendant phone calls from parents. One parent was in genuine anguish at his son securing four rather than the requisite five A-C grades in order to embark on a sixth-form A level course. Do we persist with this artificial hoop, I ask myself, in the knowledge that in three years time he can secure a university place in science with two E grades? Do we extend this logic to discourage potential English and history students unless they can be certain of A and B grades?

In a school in which this summer's GCSE science A-C grades matched almost exactly our overall A-C percentage, we have subsequently seen in students' choice of A level courses an overwhelming flight from biology and chemistry to geography and English. The wheel turns inexorably.

Meanwhile sixth-form GCSE resits told the usual tale of better to travel hopefully than arrive. During the past two decades with this 17 plus age group we have experimented with CEE, CPVE and a bevy of diplomas. We need now to make GNVQs work, together with an end to the traditional three A levels.

As a profession, let us reflect seriously on the merits of a two-year course of five or six AS levels, with the stipulation that a modern language, a science and an arts subject must be included. In this way we may perhaps conquer the Arts/Science gulf and see an end to the current follies of HE admissions procedures and the removal of the inequities which this year's struggle for university places has highlighted for thousands of youngsters.

So much for schools. What about HE?

The party conferences are examining what the state can afford as the millennium approaches: state pensions versus mortgage subsidies; child benefits versus student grants; public utilities versus private venture capital to build motorways, schools and hospitals; and so on. Our political leaders should enable us to address these decisions openly and intelligently.

In the educational sector it is no coincidence that our one private university, Buckingham, runs two-year courses, comprising a total of eight terms and starting in January. All vice-chancellors should be encouraged to study this model.

Students funding themselves through university, including tuition fees, will come sooner rather than later to the British system. The nation cannot afford otherwise and the sooner we are honest with ourselves the better for our current generation of secondary-aged children.

Faced with such costs parents and students will willingly and properly opt for two-year degrees, and there is no reason why compression of time should compromise quality. Moving to a January start would remove the August silly season of unnecessary disappointments. Sixth-form students could then be applying in the early autumn on the basis of substantive grades and more meaningful school references. Might they also be expected to use the 'gap' term for some form of locally based community service?

Meanwhile, the Government wrestles with public finances, seeking to avoid a repetition of the United States' billion dollar deficit running out of control. Schools, colleges and the examination boards are examining the 14-19 curriculum in an attempt to make it more coherent. Under these circumstances, a coming together of vested interests is not only politically feasible but essential.

If we are not to be bound in shallows and miseries well into the early decades of the 21st century, there has now to be creative, unfettered dialogue between the schools and university sectors. Our Secretary of State for Education is uniquely well placed to begin the process this autumn. In so doing he may secure his own political fortune, enhance the continuing education life-chances of future generations, and go some way towards solving not an inconsiderable part of the nation's financial troubles.

***

RAISE THE UNDERCLASS

Times Educational Supplement   *September 1996*

The long tail of underachievement continues to wag. The question is: does it wag hard enough to change the parts of our schooling system which urgently need it?

Various commentators suggest that up to 100,000 of our young people reach 16 without attaining levels that one should expect of an 11-year-old. In one urban local authority last year 41 per cent of its 11-year-olds had a reading age below nine.

The Office for Standards in Education's commissioned report *Worlds Apart?* offers depressing international comparisons, most notably highlighting the great disparity between our high and low achievers. In league table terms England has a greater proportion of low achieving pupils than our major international competitors.

Recent GCSE statistics confirm that 15 per cent of our students at 16 do not achieve at least grade G in English, and 17 per cent in mathematics, while 21 per cent fail to achieve at least a grade G in English, mathematics and science as a combination.

Last year's figures reveal that more than 46,000 16-year-olds reached the end of compulsory education without a GCSE grade. What 1996's analysis produces we await: have, as headlines claim, weaker pupils been "sacrificed in grades chase"?

Whatever the final verdict, there is no concealing the sense of abject failure, disillusion and rejection that thousands of 16-year-olds experience year on year.

Away from the headlines, the reality behind these figures have – in their hundreds of thousands across the 5-16 age range – returned to classrooms this month. For those destined not to trouble the GCSE points scorer, are we serving them at all?

Take first the home background of many children. A tour of many urban housing estates quickly uncovers a rotting social fabric which the comfortable majority would prefer not to acknowledge. A more searching analysis reveals the number of satellite dishes on the outsides of houses in inverse proportion to the numbers of books read inside them – an arresting Orwellian image that begins to explain much early language deprivation.

Poverty of aspirations is endemic, notably among young males. According to last year's Joseph Rowntree Foundation report, these are part of the bottom 10 per cent of the population whose incomes have dropped by 17 per cent in the past decade, while the top 10 per cent have increased by a staggering 61 per cent.

It was JK Galbraith who first defined the culture of contentment of the majority of America's citizens. This is a society which leaves 37 million Americans unable to afford private health care. What characterises the culture of the contented majority is threefold: its affirmation that it is receiving its just desserts; its highly selective view of the role of the state (what President Reagan and Mrs Thatcher winningly called "getting government off the backs of the people"); and its tolerance of big differences in income and achievement.

Similar divisions are being played out this side of the Atlantic. Significantly, amid pre-election jousting we see our politicians deftly side-stepping the functional underclass. The unemployed and economically inactive – a segment of the 30/30/40 society – described by Will Hutton, author of *The State We're In* – don't vote and therefore don't count. So why bother with them?

What characterises many of our urban and city-edge spaces is a cultural numbness. Blockbuster Video stores outnumber bookshops and libraries by the score. I recently visited a Midlands town serving more than 2,500 children aged 5-16 where the nearest bookshop is a John Menzies 13 miles away.

In another local authority, the director of education informed me that 45 per cent of children in the authority's schools currently come from homes where no adult is in paid employment. A recent skills audit of an ex-mining community revealed that 70 per cent of males over 44 had not worked for five years and saw little prospect of ever doing again. What kind of future does this present to their daughters and sons?

Many attempts are being made to revive the areas laid waste during the 1980s. But there is no mistaking the casual violence of life, housing, health and education in too many of these settings. To be on the wrong side of the tracks in say, Portsmouth, Leeds, Brighton, Oxford, Newcastle, or Plymouth is to be a largely forgotten voter.

In the 1970s when l was teaching near the Oval in south London a councillor friend suggested to me that the only way to improve the lot of local children was to suspend the not inconsiderable Inner London Education Authority budget for a year or two and reinvest it in housing.

His argument has stayed with me. It is a powerful reminder that that the influence of the home is paramount, that the die is cast young, that the role of parents in the education of their children continues to be under-valued by our Lottery society.

As youngsters return to their schools in these areas what does the system offer them? More than 20 years teaching in inner-city and shire comprehensives persuades me that schools can and do make a difference. Where the cocktail of effective leadership, adequate resources and exciting teaching flows, schools flourish.

But schools can only do so much. There are increasing minorities within them who never really become part of the mainstream. To take two cases I've encountered so far this term: what does a primary school do with the nine out of 28 entering reception class who do not meet the School Curriculum and Assessment Authority's desirable outcomes that "they write their names with appropriate use of upper and lower case letters" and "they recognise and use number to 10"? Or the secondary school which has identified that 72 of its 180 new entrants have a reading age more than two years below their chronological one?

The situation in which many of our schools increasingly find themselves demands more than mischievous radical thinking – a radicalism which politicians of all hues sadly dare not utter. Votes lie in the comfort zones.

With party manifestos on the horizon let me single out just four strands against which we might judge future political thinking.

Let us squarely recognise that the seeds of educational disaffection at 14-plus are sown in the experiences of early years. National and local government social policy needs to be shaped around motivating parents to value learning in the home.

Inadequate resources are an inescapable issue in the primary sector. Let every child entering reception class for whom English is a second language count double in local management funding. Such a system has operated successfully in Holland for many years. Allied to this, let government urge Private Finance Initiatives to fund afterschool study support centres in all urban primary schools, in which effective family literacy and parenting classes can take place.

For many of our children – and their non-specialist teachers – aspects of both key stage 1 and key stage 2 curriculum should be suspended to allow a focus on language and number. So-called desirable outcomes need to be a solid reality before children can access much of the primary curriculum. It is a vanity to plan otherwise.

From the start of secondary school the culture of mediocrity among pupils has to be robustly countered by teachers. The peer group pressure to under-achieve must not be allowed to set the prevailing tone. Those pupils who begin to sink need well-resourced additional support and a modified curriculum offer, thoughtfully timetabled. The fundamentals of key stage 3 are sound. Equally, let us take an honest look at what many pupils gain from, for example, a compulsory modern foreign language.

We can no longer pretend that the comprehensive enables all students to realise potential. Our European neighbours and the Asian tigers whom politicians engagingly cite have long recognised the need for alternative structures. Vocational colleges need to be introduced for upwards of 20 per cent of 14-plus students; these to include block release for paid employment. Only that way will ambitions for general national vocational qualifications and national training and education targets be realised.

Hundreds of thousands of our pupils succeed. We should acknowledge and celebrate that, especially in the face of seasonal and hasty calls for root and branch change. Many do not. Current structures and curriculum serve only to reject them. Their future years in classrooms start today; their failing experience of schooling will shape society's values and achievements into the 21st century.

We are – in some urban contexts – just one beat ahead of social breakdown: take a glance at the wrong side of the tracks in Washington DC, Orlando or Milwaukee. Schools are vital crucibles which can make a difference, but only if the reforming political will to listen to the unspoken voice of the underclass is forthcoming.

***

THE THIRD WAY

Times Educational Supplement   *July 1998*

The investment bank Goldman Sachs & Co made a record £2 billion profit last year. Its UK partners – Government advisers among them – look set to "earn" an average £60 million in projected share sales.

Within half a mile of the bank's London office is a typical inner-city primary school: outside toilets, leaky ceilings, a stockaded playground on the 19th century building's rooftop – and teachers delivering the Literacy Hour to classes of 30 pupils, a third of whom don't have English as their heritage language. To make the 10-minute walk between the two buildings is to witness first-hand an unpalatable apartheid in contemporary Britain.

The dilemma for the Government in this wicked juxtaposition of private wealth and state poverty is that it was elected on a nod and a wink from the electorate not to tax and spend.

To raise taxes for the middle-class voter is the "third rail" of British politics today: touch it and you get fried. For all the "Education, education, education" mantra, to date there is relatively little evidence of significant change in the resourcing of schools.

But does the much-heralded Third Way from the Blair Government offer the prospect of real new money for public services, especially in regions that need transforming levels of investment?

A recent seminar of Labour thinkers pragmatically concluded (perhaps predictably because it appears attractively budget-neutral) that the Third Way is "whatever works". Where in education can one look for pioneering work that in some way might help define the elusive Third Way?

My own belief is that the proposed education action zones present a unique arena for such innovation. David Blunkett's characteristically positive introduction to the Department for Education and Employment's leaflet on zones asks how areas can develop "virtuous circles" to improve the education of disadvantaged pupils. This is a telling phrase.

Critics are quick to argue that all this has been tried before: education priority areas; city technology colleges; the Private Finance Initiative. Do, then, the zones add up to a fresh start or a recasting of previous policies?

If zones are to be lighthouses of excellence in raising standards (the US Edison Project is suitably titled), then what follows must be their defining features:

In round figures today, each pupil in the state sector is "worth" £2,000; in the private sector, the figure is £5,000. In other words Torquay plays Arsenal, to use the metaphor beloved of many a Government adviser. If zones are to make any serious long-term impact, then they must close dramatically that gap by harnessing public, private-sector and charitable foundation investment in our schools system. Upon this fundamental point the rest stands or falls.

Radicalism must be the dominant hand. High-quality teacher recruitment and retention can be achieved through significantly altered pay and conditions. Essential curriculum change and innovation (for example, how learning slots are organised) will follow. The teaching force, pupil population, families and local community must be prepared to strengthen what works in an area and unequivocally eschew worn-out practice.

Sensitivity to what exists and has gone before is as vital a part of the success cocktail as the theme of radical change. Groups of headteachers, teachers and governors should feel confident that their local knowledge, intuitions and skills will count, that they will not be overthrown by some here-today-gone-tomorrow bright idea. Embedding change and sustaining the quest for excellence will be vital. Politicians will need to suspend their natural preference for short-termism.

A new culture and climate of learning should permeate the entire zone, cradle to grave. What areas now bidding to establish zones have in common are communities where under-achievement and low self-esteem are endemic. Poverty of aspiration prevails. Social exclusion is as evident on street corners as it is prevalent in Cabinet ministers' speeches.

A powerful programme for early-years, health and education must be a cornerstone. Real access to lifelong learning opportunities is a basic building block. Truancy, disruptive behaviour, boys' under-achievement, and poor literacy skills will be tackled relentlessly and creatively.

Historic definitions of the school day and the school building will be challenged. What currently appears as a disjointed plethora of out-of-school initiatives (summer literacy schemes, kids' clubs, football club study centres, teenage mentoring, early learning excellence centres, Internet classes, Bookstart for babies) will find a fresh focus. Children and their families will see that virtual or classroom education can be open all hours, 365 days of the year.

A cluster of schools will give local meaning to "subsidiarity" and "solidarity". There will be the rapid recognition of what each player can achieve alone, what the players can only achieve when working in partnership. Brave, questioning leadership will be a pre-requisite, ever searching for win-win solutions to chronic problems that will raise community expectation of what lifelong learning can deliver.

Why am I so optimistic that all this can be achieved? For the past two years I have travelled more than 50,000 miles around the UK working in areas which present contrasts of public squalor and private wealth that are, frankly, obscene.

In all of these areas there is a profound will on the part of non-profit organisations, private foundations and the business sector to invest in education – if it is done in a carefully planned and focused way. Many outstanding examples now exist – in rural and urban settings – of communities that flourish, rather than merely survive, as a result of significant corporate and charitable investment.

There is the widespread recognition that raising educational standards for all has to be a shared enterprise. It cannot be left to the formal providers of schools alone. When a company invests money and volunteer-employee time into its local community, it knows that it is making an invaluable contribution to young people's lifelong learning habits.

The wealth of our society in the late 20th century is palpably not evident in the state education system. Nor, on current public-service expenditure plans, is the state set to do anything different into the new century. That may change –we don't know yet. But government can help create the climate and the tax framework for partnership investment.

Within the next five years exciting, creative social entrepreneurs will, I believe, help define the Third Way in education. They will succeed in bringing together business corporations and private foundation to investment in the state schooling system. Action zones will prove the dawning of David Blunkett's virtuous circles.

***

LITERACY IS LIKE A VIRUS – BENIGN AND MALIGN

Independent   *21st November 2000*

From a lecture for the Royal Society of Arts

The writer Michael Ignatieff, a decade or more ago, coined the phrase "the three-minute culture". When I was working in the United States during the 1992 presidential election campaign, an optimum sound bite from a politician was 7.4 seconds long. Any longer, and the average TV viewer would take their remote control and go "click" to another channel.

In the spirit of our increasingly "takeaway" age, the takeaway moments of this talk are: firstly, literacy is like a virus, benign and malign. Raising standards of literacy is first and foremost a family responsibility – schools can do a lot but they can't do everything to create a civilised, literate society. The Jesuits had it oh so right: the early years matter. Good schools make a real difference, but they are now over-controlled, over-inspected and almost overwhelmed. Finally, teacher recruitment is the stumbling block to breaking the cycle of illiteracy in our inner-urban and edge-city areas.

From my first teaching job as a tutor of literacy in HM Prison Brixton to the present day, I have believed profoundly that literacy is about autonomy, self-esteem, power – power through language and, linked to that, having a predisposition to learn and think. My father reads the dictionary every day – he says your life depends upon your power to master words. He also says he's keeping Alzheimer's at bay! Reading is the ability to understand the thoughts and feelings of another mind via the medium of text: from *The Beano* to the Bible, from *Ulysses* to the internet. Reading is also an amplifier of human abilities. Crucially, it offers independent access to information and communication.

We need a national commission or similar on teacher recruitment; on the nature of learning in schools and beyond, and what society wants from its teachers over the coming decades. The system currently creaks, nowhere more so than where it most matters in terms of any social inclusion agenda. As Lou Reed sang in search of the perfect day: "You're going to reap just what you sow".

Building a literate nation is not about a commando raid on the inarticulate. It is about long-term investment of ideas and resources. Remember the tale of the Irish supermarket retailer Fergal Quinn who, on a visit to the US, wanted to check out a fellow-chain's claim to be "the friendliest supermarket". The chain promised that if the checkout staff didn't say "thank-you", then the customer could claim a dollar. At the check out with a few items in his shopping basket, the promised "thank you" was not forthcoming. Exuding Irish charm, he asked for his dollar, only to be told by the checkout girl, "Oh! That promotion finished last month!"

Most importantly, building the literacy profile is about forging those potent partnerships which the National Literacy Trust has devoted itself to. Yes, it is about urging public, private and non-profit sectors to value schooling and lifelong learning and make investments accordingly. Schools and teachers can't do it alone – ever. For me, it is, with hearts and minds, beginning at the beginning.

Passing on the torch of literacy from one generation to the next is centrally a family issue. If all children are to go to school with their starter-motor well oiled, then all parents should be helped to make that early investment of time, of talk and chatter and gossip – on the knee, in the bath, in bed.

A very short story to conclude. Two frogs lived on a dairy farm and fell into a churn of milk. The sides were too steep for them to climb out, and after swimming around for some time, one of them gave up the struggle and drowned. The other worked his feet to the rhythm of "With Allah's help, with Allah's help". In the morning, he was discovered exceedingly tired but perched safely on a mound of soft butter! Yes, in the end, it's all a question of faith.

***

WHAT IS THE LEGACY OF THE EDUCATION ACT, 70 YEARS ON?

The Guardian   *22nd April 2014*

Rab Butler's 1944 reforms gave teachers autonomy but schools' freedom today comes with strings attached

In March 1943, Rab Butler, the young president of the Board of Education, went to Chequers to see Winston Churchill. After a weekend of playing bagatelle, dining and watching films of Tsarist Russia, Butler found a moment alone with him. The meeting with Churchill – leaning back on his pillows in a four-poster bed, night-cap on and with a large cat at his feet – was an unlikely beginning for the most fundamental reform of the English education system, but that night the prime minister signed off on what became the 1944 Education Act.

Conceived during the Blitz and the Normandy landings, it is remarkable to think that civil servants and ministers were focused on post-war reconstruction in order to build, as they saw it, the new Jerusalem. Churchill, in one of his inimitable radio broadcasts to the nation, described the Act as "the greatest scheme of improved education that has ever been attempted by a responsible government".

Seventy years on, the legacy of the Education Act is still widely felt. Michael Barber, historian of the Act, who as head of Tony Blair's delivery unit introduced strategies and targets to the nation's classrooms, says Butler's seminal 1944 reforms would be hard to implement now. "It's very hard to do today what Butler did in the 1940s, to build a consensus and then make the change, simply because of the nature of the modern world," he says. "If you try to build a consensus now, the world moves before you've had time to do the reform."

Today we accept free primary and secondary education as a national birth-right. But pre-war, things were very different. Most pupils left school at 14. Butler's Act introduced compulsory education to 15, with a clause to raise it to 16; any fee-paying at state schools was forbidden; and church schools were brought into the national system.

So the 1944 Education Act provided real chances of social mobility, something educationalists ever since have tried to build on.

But passing the 11-plus didn't necessarily guarantee working-class pupils would take up their place at grammar school. Baroness Shirley Williams, who was education secretary between 1976 and 1979, says: "I had several friends whose parents couldn't afford the uniform," she says. "They never went to grammar school at all. Others didn't go because they were expected to stay until at least 15 and their parents wanted them to come out as quickly as possible to get jobs."

A documentary broadcast on Radio 4 tonight explores the legacy of Butler's Act, and finds an education system where all too often the government of the day was pitted against the teaching profession. Williams, in the 1970s, like subsequent education secretaries, felt the displeasure of the teaching profession at close quarters. "Going to education conferences was to be crucified," recalls Williams. "You got spat at, you got shouted at, you got abuse hurled at you."

The 1944 Education Act had established a national education system, but with the power to implement change delegated to local education authorities and revered chief officers, such as Alec Clegg in the West Riding of Yorkshire, who toured the county, inspiring teachers and making it clear who ran education in his area. This was an era of considerable teacher autonomy and little accountability to parents. Today, ministers argue, this autonomy has been resurrected: after the New Labour years of targets and centrally driven strategies, teachers can once again teach as they choose in return for greater accountability. And the appointment this month of a high-powered team of regional commissioners to oversee academies is reminiscent of Butler's vision for local chief officers. But since 1944, successive governments have also shown they cannot resist pulling power to Whitehall. What Kenneth Baker, David Blunkett and Michael Gove have devolved with one hand, they have taken back to the centre with the other.

Butler's legacy remained relatively unscathed until Kenneth Baker's 1988 Education Reform Act, which dismantled much of what he had created, with directives from Whitehall about curriculum and testing, the birth of GCSEs and the advent of local management of schools, which challenged the historic role of local authorities. Now headteachers and governors had control of their budgets, and teachers naturally became nervous of pay and conditions being worked out by individual schools rather than through national agreements.

But if Baker was controlling, Blair and Blunkett were even more centrist and interventionist when they delivered the "Education, education, education" mantra in 1997. Where the Butler Act was localist, New Labour actively challenged schools' autonomy through targets, strategies and league tables, which overwhelmed the profession. Relations with the teaching unions hit a nadir, with ballots and strikes in the late 1990s. Blunkett is unapologetic: "If you're going to bring about change, you're going to break eggs, and the grump in the staffroom was always going to have one foot in the grave," he says.

Today, Michael Gove seems just as happy to incur the wrath of teachers. Sir David Bell, permanent secretary at the Department for Education under both Labour and coalition governments, tells the programme: "There was clearly a quite significant attempt by the coalition government to reset the relationship with the trade unions."

Despite all the criticisms of academies, free schools and excessive testing of pupils, schools are unquestionably better places to be than in 1944. There is now investment in state education which Butler and Churchill could only have dreamed about. And while social-mobility challenges persist, university participation has risen in a way the reformers in 1944 could not have imagined.

What will the education system look like in 70 years' time? Blunkett, who has been reviewing education policy for Labour, is clear about his party's next steps. "I think the changes are irreversible," he says, "although we'll want to build on them and we'll want to reintroduce the glue." So he is rejecting the idea of thousands of schools working alone, preferring a rejuvenation in counties or regions of ambitious and inspiring political and headteacher leaders: "Academies are here to stay, but we need something like the Cleggs of West Yorkshire rather than the Cleggs of the modern era."

National politicians since 1944 have been unable to resist tinkering with and sometimes meddling in the nation's classrooms. Greater autonomy has often felt like it has come with conditions attached – you are free to run your own schools as long as you do it the way we want you to. At times, teachers have responded naively and crudely – Gove is certainly not the first education secretary to bring them out of the classroom on to the street in protest.

The story since 1944 has been one of conflict and consensus, with varying degrees of intensity. What is needed is mutual trust in education: between central government and teachers, and between local and national politicians. The successful future of our schools is one in which governments meddle less, and trust more. And teachers demonstrate an altogether new professionalism.

***

Acknowledgements

When asked to describe my own style and approach as a writer, I place myself partly in the camp of Shakespeare's character Autolycus in *The Winter's Tale*: a 'snapper-up of unconsidered trifles'.

One of my first editors at the *Times Educational Supplement* during the 1970s told me there was no such thing as a copyright on ideas. He also advised helpfully against what he called 'too much subjectivity in your phrasing'. Writers of fiction and non-fiction alike absorb a range of influences through their experiences and reading, and then seek to create texts and narratives in their own image.

I once interviewed the English author Jeffrey Archer to be told by that master storyteller that there are but four plots in the whole of world literature, pivoted upon love, hate, power and betrayal. The writer must make of these what he can.

'A Reading Tale' (Chapter 14) offers a list of books whose ideas have absorbed me as a reader and teacher, and have influenced my writing. From these and many other published sources I have doubtless borrowed some felicitous phrasing, wittingly or unwittingly. With the advent of the internet we are all ethical plagiarists now. We all stand on the shoulders of those giants who wrote before us.

I should like to recognise here the influences of all those with whom I have worked in schools and many other settings, and those whom I've taught. As a teacher, intermittent encounters with former pupils are inescapable experiences. I've enjoyed my share, but to protect the great and the fallen amongst them, they remain anonymous, at least in this book.

Leading the National Education Trust over the past eight years has brought me into contact with an unparalleled array of dynamic practitioners, writers and thinkers across the world whose work and dangerous ideas have made an impression on *The Restless School*. I warmly acknowledge these too.

I record here my particular appreciation to the Trustees and staff of the National Education Trust, UK for affording me time to complete this book. And to John Catt Educational, who keep the publishing process gloriously nimble.

Finally, my thanks to family, friends and colleagues who have been part of my school journey to date, 1957 – 2014.

Roy Blatchford

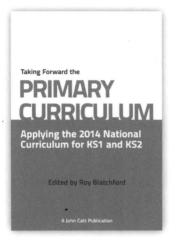

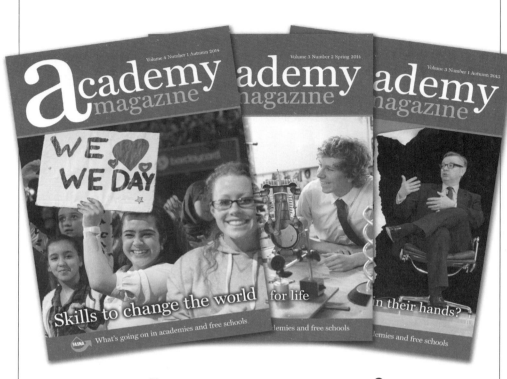